BANGKOK BOY

BANGKOK BOY

The Story of a Stolen Childhood

Chai Pinit

In the interest of privacy, all names have been changed. Any resemblance to persons living or dead is purely coincidental.

PUBLISHED IN 2008 BY MAVERICK HOUSE PUBLISHERS.
Maverick House, Office 19, Dunboyne Business Park, Dunboyne,
Co. Meath, Ireland.
Maverick House Asia, Level 43, United Centre, 323 Silom Road,
Bangrak, Bangkok 10500, Thailand.

info@maverickhouse.com
http://www.maverickhouse.com

ISBN: 978-1-905379-51-4

5 4 3 2 1

The paper used in this book comes from wood pulp of managed forests. For every tree felled, at least one tree is planted, thereby renewing natural resources.

The moral rights of the authors have been asserted.

A CIP catalogue record for this book is available from the British Library.

ACKNOWLEDGEMENTS

My utmost appreciation goes to Soshan Itsarachon for without you this book would never have come into being. You spent months patiently interviewing me, seeking me out during some of the lowest points of my life as a true friend, forcing me to face the truth about myself. Also thanks to all at Maverick House.

INTRODUCTION

I awake slowly and painfully. Where am I?

A hospital ward it seems.

Bedridden, and in extreme agony, I lie motionless. Two things are certain: my skull is throbbing with pain, and my heart is caught in a vice-like grip of terror. As I examine my bloodied hand assessing the damage, I struggle to recall where it all went so terribly wrong.

The last thing I remember is drinking with friends— for the past 25 years this is almost the only thing I have done, so it's not a helpful memory. I vaguely remember a fight breaking out, although fighting has also been a customary pasttime, so again it doesn't explain much.

Here I am in hospital again, and in hell once again. I cannot believe it. I learn that I've been in a coma and am lucky to be alive. I don't feel lucky, although I realise that I probably don't deserve to be alive. I am like a cat with nine lives, but I'd say I'm on my eighth life already.

The few memories I have are sketchy at best, but they are enough to make me realise that I have to change my life if I want to live. And being so close to death has made me realise that I *do* want to live. It's like a lightbulb being switched on for me.

Despite my injuries, my mind is active—in fact, it's a whirlpool of distressed commotion. How did I lose myself, who have I become, and how can I find my way back? I rack my brain for clues as to where my life began to go wrong. How could I have changed so drastically from being a promising, carefree country boy into this man with no future at all?

These questions play over and over in my head. I'm tormented by them. I feel like I'm drowning. Distraught, I'm entrapped in a waking nightmare.

One thing is certain: no matter how many painkillers I'm given, they will never assuage the anguish caused by the knowledge that I have been living a complete lie. I've gone to ridiculous lengths to hide the damage, the pain and emptiness, of a life lived in the shadow of abuse—abuse suffered at the hands of others and myself.

We Thais believe that a newborn child is a white piece of cloth that will be sullied over time by life's misdeeds. My white-cloth days were so few I can scarcely remember them. How could something so pure and innocent to begin with become so repulsive?

I was an ordinary boy who liked nothing more than to make his parents proud. That innocent child is now a complete stranger.

If I'm honest, I know my decline began long ago. I was a teenager when I was first sexually abused by a teacher. Later, my spirituality was violated at the hands of a 'holy' man—my abbot. I was cleverly coerced into giving up my body for the perverse pleasure of others; yet I willingly traded my innocence in return for treats and money—pittances that in my naiveté I considered treasured goods. These experiences then spawned a series of sordid life choices that warped my reality.

I developed despicable personality traits that were nonetheless necessary if I was to survive in this fallen world. These very traits came close to extinguishing the life I sought to preserve.

I worked as a male sex worker, which satiated my selfish desires and temporarily masked the pain that naturally results from such employment. In an attempt to regain some control over my life, I became a slave to addictions such as drinking, gambling, and a constant desire for other prostitutes.

I've demeaned myself by performing in the worst kinds of pornography imaginable. I've watched many friends die, some as victims of AIDS; and I have even secured young boys to gratify the same type of monstrous men who once led me astray.

Foolishly, I passed up opportunities that could have granted me a better life. Instead I plunged into the lowest depths to which anyone can possibly descend.

I fear my death is near, but I don't want to end my life like this. I wish to tell my story. I NEED to tell my story. I sense that if I don't, I'll fall through the cracks and all memory of me will be lost forever. My story is not an easy one to share, nor is it a pleasant one to read. I don't ask for pity from those who are privy to the dark secrets that have entrapped me for so long. By immersing myself in the putrid cesspool of my past, I hope to find my way out and gain a semblance of freedom. Perhaps you, my companions, can learn from my mistakes, and then my life will not have been lived in vain.

CHAPTER 1

My father Liang was a minor celebrity in Sisaket Province in the northeast region of Thailand called Isan. He earned a reputation as a tough guy both by his association with notorious mafia-type characters and through his years of involvement in professional Muay Thai kickboxing. During his twenties, he won various prize fights and supplemented his income by working as a brothel bouncer. My father was generous to a fault when it came to his friends for he regularly plied them with money and booze. Given that he worked in a field dominated by macho men, it's not surprising that he fell in with criminals and other dubious characters. He believed their company earned him 'face', protection, and respect from the community, and he was later to instil this harmful mentality in me.

During his stint in the construction industry, Pa worked in a Buddhist temple in a remote village in Sisaket. He promptly became enchanted by a local beauty named Phikun, who would later bear him five children. I was the auspicious firstborn male and they named me Chai, which means 'victory' in Thai. Pa often proudly recounted how he and my mother first met.

Apparently their union had been the talk of the village. In those days, a good-looking worldly boxer falling in love with a peasant woman was a fairytale romance. The female villagers evaluated prospective husbands by their ability to provide financial security, and were green-eyed with jealousy over my mother landing on her feet in such a manner.

The fact that my Pa was of Chinese descent, and that he already had a Chinese wife, made his interracial relationship with my mother all the more romantic. However, Pa's family discouraged him from taking a Thai woman as a minor wife because they believed that a Chinese woman should fill the role. Despite their protests, he moved from town to my mother's village, sat an exam to become a primary-school teacher and set up a home with her, leaving his wild past behind.

Before Pa moved in with Mae he spent most of his time with his posse of thugs, all of whom had eagerly done his bidding. Over the years, most of them were shot dead by the police following a series of vigilante crackdowns. Although Pa was tough he was never convicted of any crimes. I guess he managed to keep a low profile and avoid the authorities' attention. In hindsight, the relocation to Mae's village probably saved him. He found a new way of life and an escape route from inevitable doom.

Pa relished in regaling us about his wilder days, telling us stories of his near-fatal left hook having knocked out opponents both inside and outside of the boxing ring. Even after settling into a quieter life, Pa still enjoyed hanging out with his thug friends. In his spare time, he taught me Muay Thai and instructed me to punch anyone who dared tease me about my small stature. He didn't see anything wrong with men settling a disagreement by force.

Pa might have been small in stature like me but was a larger-than-life character. When I was a boy, he imparted many tips on what it meant to be a *chai chatri*, or 'real man'. He told me that the best way to keep one's cronies under control was to provide them with free liquor, cigarettes, money and food. He believed respect was a commodity that could be bought for a price. He certainly possessed a lot of face amongst the simple-thinking folk of our area. In my village, people often took the law into their own hands and some would behave as if they were above it. Fights frequently erupted amongst the young testosterone-crazed gangs. Men would be quick to aim a gun at the competition if a girl's heart was at stake. In fact, it didn't take much to provoke someone into using a weapon. People were often well lubricated by copious amounts of *lao khao*, a strong, locally produced rice wine, so emotions ran high. Most villagers didn't possess many valuables; however, 'face' was the one virtue everyone strove to acquire and maintain. Men seemed to be particularly guarded when it came to this. Pa's rule was simple: he would be civil to anyone so long as they respected him in return.

My father's macho persona aside, I looked up to him, and worshipped the ground he walked upon. In

1967, before I was born, my parents set up a successful grocery store in our house. Being a natural leader and showman, Pa devoted himself to endeavours benefiting the community. In the provinces, teachers are greatly respected and admired and are viewed as second parents to the children. Such civil service jobs offer not only stability but also a pension, and even access to welfare-programme loans that are exclusively designed for government officials.

Pa unofficially claimed the leadership of his community and was generous and respectful to everyone who sought his help. He gained the support of a healthcare programme by using his position as a teacher to encourage villagers to have their blood tested to prevent malarial epidemics. Whenever someone knocked at our shop door seeking to purchase alcohol in the early hours of the morning, he gladly got up and served them. It never occurred to him that these off-hours dealings might invite a burglar into our home. He sold goods on credit to some of the more destitute neighbours and acted as a moneylender to others. Pa's good deeds earned him a huge amount of face. To this day, I'm intrigued by the combination of tough and gentle qualities that made Pa the man he was.

My father's major weakness was a terrible dependence on alcohol. This problem came to a head after he was badly injured in a motorcycle accident whilst driving under the influence. It was the last straw for Mae and she gave him an ultimatum. She demanded he sober up by undergoing an ordination ritual with a local spiritual medium. Either that or he would never see her again.

As a prerequisite for laymen wishing to become a *khon song chao*, or 'medium', he or she must abide by Buddha's five precepts. The fifth precept forbids the ingestion of any substance that could cause a loss of consciousness. Consequently, my father was required to stop drinking for a period of time before presenting himself to the *khru*, or 'master', to begin his training. Having accomplished this feat, he sought a renowned medium who would agree to take him on as an apprentice. He presented his chosen master with candles, incense, flowers, a small amount of money, and a piece of white cloth as a gesture of respect.

Having undergone the ordination ritual, it was believed that my father returned home with a higher spirit accompanying him. Pa invited the spirit to reside in a holy room (*hong phra*) in our house where we kept Buddhist and Hindu statues such as those of Brahma and Indra. He'd visit this room daily and make small offerings while chanting various mantras in an effort to retain the favour of these higher spirits. In his spare time he took to predicting the fortunes of villagers who sought to safeguard themselves from possible tragedy, adding yet another title to his diverse portfolio. Sadly, my father only stayed sober long enough to see the birth of his fifth and final child; after that he promptly returned to the bottle and my mother gave up all hope of ever seeing him sober again.

After witnessing the influence that spiritualism had on my father, my mother's faith began to blossom and she resolved to become a serious medium herself. She not only made a name for herself in the village but even surpassed my father's capabilities. Seekers came to our house from near and far in search of cures for ailments that doctors had failed to diagnose. Some brought loved ones who suffered from serious inertia and depression, believing them to be caused by a curse or a bad spirit. One woman in particular had been rendered catatonic by a mysterious force. My mother divined that a guardian tree spirit had laid claim to her soul. She had apparently offended it while picking mushrooms in the forest, during which time she stopped to answer the call of nature by an old tree. But this was the tree in which a supposed spirit dwelt, and it was provoked by this act to take revenge. Through my mother's gift of healing the woman was delivered from the clutches of the tree spirit, and restored to a normal, emotionally healthy state. While channelling higher spirits, Mae played the part of spiritual medium fully by draping a white cloth over her shoulders. Her power to remove such curses was said to be granted by way of chanting mantras in the ancient Khmer language.

Besides this, Mae handled countless other cases such as those involving people who were convinced their enemies had enlisted the services of a sorcerer to cast black-magic spells on them. The sorcerer used tools that included a hay voodoo doll representing the unwitting target. He would command tormented spirits who'd died in unfortunate accidents to plague the target with all sorts of indefinable and incurable ailments. With the use of a consecrated knife, he could even bind, for better or for worse, two souls together forever.

Mae was very successful and her acclaim occasionally took her to other provinces to perform exorcisms. She earned good money from this work and developed a devout following. Unfortunately, most of her money was eaten up by her gambling and by the five hungry mouths of her children. Like my father, she was very indulgent and couldn't bear to refuse her offspring anything.

Mae never hinted that her reputed powers were a sham. Up to her dying day she remained genuinely convinced of her channelling abilities. Regardless of what secrets she might or might not have been harbouring, I greatly admired her for the fact that she managed to make such a reputation for herself despite her lack of education. People used to call to our house/grocery store/medium centre around the clock. It was a one-stop shop for nearly every physical and spiritual need imaginable.

By Western standards my family would have been considered poor; but according to the standards of rural Thailand we were quite well off. We never had to beg for food or buy goods on credit like many of our neighbours; and aside from the grocery store, we also had a storage house, an orchard, and rice paddies that were dotted across the land we owned. Whatever I wanted, I could usually find in our grocery store or get it from my parents who would give me money. I knew the various hiding places they used to stash away their money, such as in pillows or jars, or buried beneath our storage house. Mae believed that it was safer to divide our savings in case thieves broke in, chances being they'd discover only one stash and we wouldn't be left baht-less. My father's approach on the other hand was to gruffly challenge imaginary bandits to raid us if they dared, because he'd be lying in wait with a gun at the ready to blow their heads off. The nearest bank was several kilometres from our village, so it could take half a day just to complete a simple deposit. Doing so also involved the risk of being ambushed by robbers along the way. So hiding the money and relying on Pa's hubris was definitely the best alternative.

My parents were generally conceited about their status and they enjoyed showing off whenever possible. Given that I studied at the school in which my father taught, I could easily have accompanied him there on his motorcycle. Instead, he insisted on buying me a quad bike to ride—I was just eight years old at the time. I haughtily sped by my poor schoolmates as they walked or peddled their rundown bicycles, hoping to make it in time for the morning National Anthem. My parents always made sure I had large notes in my wallet when realistically all I really needed was a few baht to pay for my lunch and the odd snack. Such displays of extravagance were just a few of the ways in which my parents earned face.

As the eldest son, I had the responsibility of excelling at everything I did, both for my own sake and for that of my parents. If I did well, it would reflect positively on them, boosting their reputations. My father instilled in my young mind that a good education was my main priority in life. Given my enterprising background, it wasn't surprising that I excelled in mathematics and often got straight A's on my report cards. I also developed my business skills by bringing sweets to school from our grocery store and selling them to my schoolmates for personal profit. Also, I was often elected class head and the teachers frequently entrusted me with extra responsibilities. Although I was a high achiever, I was by no means the teacher's pet, and although I generally got along well with the boys, I was less successful with the girls. I thought they were peculiar creatures and I rarely interacted with them.

After school, my father regularly assigned extra homework and I wasn't allowed to go out to play until I'd completed it. Strangely enough, I didn't feel any pressure to be a good boy; rather, I was naturally inclined to want to make my parents proud.

Our one-storey house was large and I often helped Mae with the chores, after which I was rewarded with coins and notes. From a young age, I was used to seeing and handling large sums of money. In the absence of meaningful conversations and guidance, I began to believe that the ability to provide for others was an important expression of love. To be fair, my parents were affectionate, but had they known the problematic relationship I would later develop with money, they would have undoubtedly been more austere and less indulgent. They meant no harm, but the fact is that they spoilt me terribly. I never had to work in the rice fields after school like other less fortunate children. Instead, my parents employed farmers to carry out this labour while I read books, played with friends, and fished in the various ponds around my village. I'd cast my fishing net and lazily recline in the hammock I'd strung up between two trees; I would then while away the time reading books or watching ants busily going about their business, while the birds sang cheerfully overhead. When the sound of fish fighting to wriggle free from the net awoke me from my blissful reverie, I'd gleefully pull in the catch of snakeheads, catfish, anabases or barbs.

While my early life was idyllic in many ways, it was not as sheltered as one might think. I craved adventure and derived great pleasure from participating in daring games. From a young age, I revelled in the sense of belonging. My group consisted solely of boys, and our games were very true to our gender. Brandishing slingshots and stones, we hunted poor unsuspecting birds and then proudly brought them home to be cooked and eaten. We made 'bullets' out of small balls of clay that we would lay out to dry in the sun until they were sufficiently hardened. Armed and ready for war, we divided into two teams, firing our 'bullets' in an effort to defeat the opposition. While we had a lot of fun, many injuries were also incurred. Sometimes, we would get carried away and substitute clay bullets with actual stones to maximise the damage. 'War' was an aggressive and adrenaline-charged game but thankfully, no eyes were ever lost.

Although I spent a lot of time with my peers, I was also fond of solitude. My favourite solo activity was hunting small lizards which required serious concentration and dexterity. I'd make whistling and clucking sounds to lure my prey down from the safety of the trees. The second they curiously poked their little heads into view, I'd capture them with a small hand-made rope noose. I often trekked into the forest in search of wild produce such as mushrooms and bamboo shoots, which I triumphantly brought home to Mae along with the birds and lizards I'd ensnared. Mae transformed my bountiful catches into delicious spicy salads, or fried them with basil leaves into my favourite dish. The most exotic treat I could hope to procure was an insect called *maeng gut chi*, which was to be found in the droppings of buffaloes. Once extracted and cleaned, it would be ground in a mortar, sprinkled with herbs, and then quickly devoured. In times of drought, we boys dug up root plants such as taro and cassava, which we ate as less desirable substitutes for rice.

My childhood certainly was blissfully innocent. As I recount it here, it feels like the fragments of someone else's life.

Despite my innocence, in my early years I developed a very self-centred outlook that made me very proud and arrogant. My parents contributed to this by making no secret of the fact that they favoured me over my siblings; especially my father, who seemed intent on moulding me in his image. In both the Chinese and Thai cultures, being the eldest son is a privileged and enviable position. Parents tend to invest the bulk of their hopes and dreams in their firstborn son to help him achieve success.

I was something of a model child whom the other parents used as an example to their errant children. My father assured me that if I continued in this vein I was destined to become a distinguished educator or a high-ranking civil servant, thus even surpassing his own achievements. Outperforming one's parents was considered a great accomplishment: we even have a term for it—*aphichattabut*.

Although teachers are respected, I considered the profession boring. Who wants to spend their days policing large groups of children? Certainly not me, that was for sure. I desired a bigger better-paid job. Before I knew it, my arrogance ballooned out of all control. I insulted fellow classmates when they didn't perform as well as me by rudely informing them that they had the brains of fish. It didn't take much for an impressionable young boy to become big-headed when all he ever heard was constant praise.

CHAPTER 2

Adolescence is a confusing period for most, and I was no different. I found myself struggling with a new attraction towards girls. Up to this point, I had only interacted with them in the classroom. I had never had a girl as a close friend, let alone been intimate with one. I became overwhelmed by my increasing attraction to these peculiar creatures. My body tensed the very second I began to talk to them and I began experiencing massive sexual urges for which I had no outlet. Sex education was unheard of back then and this left me ill-equipped to deal with these changes. Adults mistakenly believed that by openly talking about the facts of life they would encourage adolescent promiscuity, so the topic was extremely taboo. Instead, we would leak misleading information among ourselves—like the blind leading the blind.

Looking back, it makes sense that my first sexual experience was with another boy. Anan, one of my closest friends, initiated our journey into this unknown amatory world. We had been chatting in my family's storage house in the middle of our big orchard when suddenly, without warning, Anan began rubbing me through my shorts. He then unzipped them and started to fondle my penis until it became hard. In the past, he had already teasingly grabbed my private parts, as boys often do in jest; however, this time he had a hungry look, and his fondling was more deliberate and serious. He clumsily began to undress me—I didn't know what to expect. I became highly aroused and completely yielded to his advances. So I helped him take off my remaining garments. He then rubbed his naked body against mine, making sure to focus particular attention on the contact of our genitalia. We squirmed excitedly and in unison as we stroked each other's penises until we both ejaculated. I was 13-years-old.

Not long after, I found another outlet to deal with my sexual urges via *chak wao*, or 'flying a kite.' This name for masturbation is derived from the repetitive motion of letting the string pass in and out of your hands as you fly a kite. With the help of pornographic magazines, my friends and I secretly competed to see who'd climax first. The most exciting *chak wao* experiences took place in the classroom. I lusted after Sai, a beautiful female teacher in her twenties who often wore fitting shirts and short skirts. She never seemed to notice her power to distract me as I stared at her beautiful smooth thighs. My fierce desires didn't go unnoticed by Khomsan, a close friend whose desk was beside mine. He would stealthily reach under the table, take hold of my erect member, and begin to rub it. I tried to remain calm and exhibit a nonchalant expression as he deftly worked my penis through my school shorts. He had me so worked up that it never took long for Khomsan to reach his goal.

Shortly before turning 14 I started seeing Sirin, my first girlfriend. She left a crumpled letter in my desk drawer, describing a dream she had about us playing together in a shallow creek near our school. Sirin was a conservative girl, yet the dream note, while innocent, was also suggestive. Looking at her budding breasts and delicate, nubile features, I found myself consumed with desire. I'd grown tired of *chak wao* and I wanted Sirin to be my first lover. But although I was filled with desire, I never so much as touched her, and this was only because I didn't know the first thing about male-female interactions.

One summer, I was asked to house-sit during the school break for my paternal grandparents in downtown Sisaket while they were on business in another province. By then, my father had reconciled with his parents over his relationship with Mae. Ama and Agong were a big part of my life and had always been extremely kind to me. The house became a popular gathering place for my friends. Loed, one of our teachers who was in his thirties, used to frequently ride his motorcycle over to visit us. He would always come bearing gifts such as *som tam* (a type of papaya salad), grilled chicken, sticky rice, and money.

My friends warned me jokingly by calling him a *tut*, which was a slang term for an effeminate man.

However, they would also call him *tua dut,* slang for a man who sucks another man's penis. So I knew exactly what these visits might entail. Surprisingly, a few of them boasted that they'd been to his house looking to release their pent-up sexual energy, and make money in the process. Apparently, he gave each boy one hundred baht per visit, which was a big amount of money for a country teenager at the time. My friends joked, 'Don't worry. You won't get pregnant! There'll be no evidence! It is a win/win situation. The teacher gets what he wants and so do we!'

He courted us as a group and befriended us in a caring manner; then he began to single us out one by one, inviting us to his place.

When it was my turn to be summoned to Loed's, he quickly ordered me to undress, shower, and wait for him in the bedroom. I quaked at the thought of what was about to transpire. I considered making a run for it, but I was overwhelmed with curiosity and desire at the thought of him performing fellatio on me. My friends had informed me of his unique talents while leaving many blanks unfilled, thus creating a longing in me to find out what was so good. In addition, I didn't want to have to later confess to my friends that I'd chickened out. In my heart I knew it was wrong for a grown man to act in this way with me, a 15-year-old, but nevertheless I awkwardly lay down on the bed and waited. Loed positioned himself beside me and started stroking my penis expertly. I didn't reciprocate as I was paralysed by guilt and fear. He then began to masturbate himself, before lowering his head to pleasure me with his mouth. I squeezed my eyes shut wanting to concentrate on the pleasure itself and not on the source of it. I became aroused. The sensation became intense; it was as if electrical currents were racing through my body. With every touch, my muscles contracted and twisted in absolute delight. He was bringing me a form of sensual gratification that I had never experienced.

At one point I took a peek at Loed and realised the reality of the situation—an effeminate teacher was molesting me. Not wanting to lose the sensations he provided, I pulled back emotionally and began to think about Sai, my sexy, short-skirted teacher. I imagined it was her luscious lips that were wrapped around my manhood, and with that I exploded into his mouth.

After he finished, Loed dressed and handed me my clothes.

'I like your facial expressions.'

I wasn't sure what he meant at first.

'The way your eyelids fluttered while I was satisfying you . . . I liked it a lot,' he continued.

He then reached into the pocket of his trousers and pulled out a small bundle of notes.

'Here's 100 baht for visiting me. No one is to know about this though. It's our secret. Whenever you need money you're welcome to come over!'

I took the money and left his house feeling pleased with myself. This tenuous connection to an adult made me feel important somehow.

Over the following years, whenever we wanted money for nice meals, cigarettes, alcohol, or movie tickets, we paid Loed a visit. We found it both freakish and amusing that a grown man was so attracted to young boys. Looking back on those visits, I can't really say that the teacher molested me because I remember the incidents as being more like business transactions. I was never attracted to Loed, but continued to see him and simply filled my mind with images of beautiful girls while he fondled me. I know that it was definitely wrong of him to take advantage of me, but then again, you can't clap with one hand; I can't deny that I was a participant. Perhaps these experiences contributed to how disastrously my life eventually turned out. It does seem plausible that there's a link between my later career choices and those early transactions with my so-called teacher.

Sin, a boy in my coterie of friends, became a regular partner of another male teacher named Pisut from our school. Unlike Loed, who rotated his affections, Pisut had a monogamous arrangement with Sin who confided that he was liked because he was well-endowed. Like the rest of us, Sin looked on the arrangement as a business deal, and one from which he made a handsome profit. Sadly, none of us took into account the incalculable cost all this was incurring to our innocence.

You could say that my village was somewhat lawless. Occasionally men were killed and women raped—all off the record, naturally. Family members or witnesses of such crimes rarely approached the police because they were afraid of being labelled a traitor. Even when they did have the courage to make a report to the police, they weren't very helpful afterwards, preferring not to get involved. The criminals in question were usually gang members who nobody wanted to mess with, and the practice of turning a blind eye only emboldened them.

Knowing that injustices wouldn't be dealt with, a group of villagers took action after a gunman killed a prominent citizen in broad daylight. They chased the offender down in the street and savagely attacked him, before turning him over to the police and thus forcing them to press charges.

To me, the police were amongst the worst wrongdoers. Growing up, I heard stories, whispered over drinks, of policemen raping village women and others they'd taken into custody. Others would blatantly abuse their position by asking girls to sleep with them. These girls often consented either out of fear or because of an ambition to become a policeman's wife. The police were also notorious for helping the big guys cover up their tracks and for accepting bribes in return for making 'it' all go away—whatever 'it' might be.

Many of the villagers owned M16s. From a young age, I was privy to the details of the weapons smuggling along the Thai/Cambodian border. Thai merchants developed relationships with the Khmer Rouge by trading legal goods in order to open the way for other dealings. Once a sense of trust had been established, the Cambodians began selling guns to the Thais—mind you, many of these same weapons had originally been sold to the Cambodians by other Thais. Such weapons were readily available and cheap, and were sometimes even traded for liquor and cigarettes. Those who couldn't afford the real deal made do with homemade rifles. Thanks to my mother, I was able to speak Khmer before I learnt to speak either Isan—the northeastern dialect, or Thai, our official language. My mother was of pure Cambodian descent, yet she'd been born in Thailand so she considered herself Thai. But she had the foresight to teach me basic Khmer in case I ever did business with our neighbours. In fact, the villagers usually conversed in Khmer and Isan rather than Thai.

Security along the border was lax at best and nonexistent at worse. The Khmer Rouge and the Thais could travel freely into each other's territory. My own village lay in close proximity to two Cambodian camps in which the inhabitants were a wild bunch. During New Year celebrations and other occasions, instead of fireworks, rounds of ammunition would be shot into the air. Under normal circumstances, Thais were generally civil to the Cambodians who shared their border.

I saw the Khmer Rouge as normal folk in every respect except for one—I was convinced they had enormous stashes of guns hidden in their bases. I accompanied my father to these villages on a number of occasions when he had produce to sell to them. They were in the process of trying to fight back Heng Samrin's soldiers, yet their camp was always open and unguarded. I witnessed many boys my own age carrying guns that were bigger than themselves. In my naiveté I thought they looked cool.

Occasionally fighting broke out on the Cambodian side between the Khmer Rouge and Heng Samrin's soldiers. My classmates, hearing volleys of gunshots being exchanged, would glibly joke that surely it was only a matter of time before the artillery found its way over to us.

My parents owned a large plot of land, which was given to them by my maternal grandparents. They had occupied the land, having been among the earliest settlers in my village. Mae's father had earned himself the nickname 'Tiger' on account of his desperado lifestyle. He was once a member of a bandit gang that made regular forays across Phanom Dongrak Mountain, into Cambodia. They would loot Cambodian villages and take whatever they could carry off with them, from fermented fish to cash.

Many of my grandfather's friends were either killed or jailed over the years. On one particular looting mission, one of Ta's friends was killed by a Cambodian sniper, causing Ta to abandon the criminal lifestyle long before I was born. He initially occupied a vast area of land but he gradually sold it off over the years at a very small profit. The land's infertility, the poor roads leading to it, and bad irrigation ensured that no great financial earnings were to be had.

I don't remember Ta being the criminal type, but rather as a conscientious worker who tended his jute farm right up to the day he passed away peacefully at the age of 84. Having Ta as a father probably explained why my mother was willing to marry a man with a shady background—she didn't grow up in a law-abiding family at all. The family's wild streak clearly rubbed off on her because once, in a fit of rage, she chased my father with a butcher's knife after she found out that he'd cheated on her with a younger woman. Fortunately, nobody was hurt and my father eventually came out of hiding. He pleaded her for forgiveness, claiming that as a man it was only natural for him to want other women.

'That's what men do,' he said.

At the front of our grocery store we had a bamboo bench and a table where customers were free to sit and enjoy themselves while drinking rice wine. Books and teachers at school all claimed drinking was a terrible vice, yet as a child my impression of alcohol was that it bound people together in happiness. Drinking and gambling were the main sources of entertainment for farmers during the dry season when farm work ceased, and my family was no exception.

I wonder if a tendency towards certain addictions is genetic because my father's father was also a heavy gambler. Unfortunately, I've far surpassed my entire family in terms of addiction. My first taste of gambling came when I was about ten years old. I took great pride in beating the adults at games of chess on which bets were always placed. At the time, it was more the adrenaline charge of winning that drew me towards betting rather than the financial reward. My parents loved to play the underground lottery and *muay tu*, which were the televised boxing matches. The TV station Channel 7 used to broadcast live kickboxing matches and villagers would place their bets on either the red or the blue fighter. This type of game was a particular crowd-pleaser, and neighbours would congregate in front of our TV set, drinking and smoking heavily while they heartily cheered.

I gradually began to lose interest in playing chess—it was too slow-paced. So instead I started playing cards in a local gambling den. My parents never warned me against following in their footsteps. They didn't consider themselves heavy gamblers as they never spent a lot of money at one time. Instead, they lost small amounts but over a long period. They claimed they only played for fun and as a way of passing the time.

Gambling greatly contributed to my obsession with money. The more I lost, the more I wanted to play to win it back. I saw money as a source of power and an excuse to show off. I developed a cocky habit of counting thick piles of banknotes in public places so that people could see how much I had. In the school canteen, while queuing for my seven-baht meal, I'd nonchalantly flip through a wad of banknotes. Money made me feel superior to both teachers and friends. When asked where the money had come from, I would boast that I'd won it in the gambling den. This was a complete lie because I generally lost far more than I ever won. It was almost impossible to beat the house; so to stay afloat I 'borrowed' money from the cash box in my family's grocery store.

To substantiate my claims, I would buy schoolmates meals and snacks. All the while, my teachers would watch on disapprovingly, but I interpreted their reaction as mere jealousy. I was persuaded by the behaviour of the likes of Loed and Pisut that, like them, all teachers harboured dirty secrets. So they had no right whatsoever to judge me.

My friends, who praised me for my generosity, fed my ego all the more. I foolishly thought the friendships were genuine and failed to see what an idiot I was—all it took was a few false compliments and I readily parted with my money. It's only now that I understand the real reason for my teachers' disapproving looks—they were looking at a good boy transforming into one that was pathetic and deluded.

Even though my parents' grocery store sold alcohol, it wasn't until my mid-teens, and after I had met Loed, that I started to become dependent on it. I frequented dens where gambling and drinking went hand in hand, just like sticky rice and chilli paste.

Noi, an older boy from the same village, recruited me into his gang of ruffians. I didn't think twice about befriending him or his fellow members. I considered it perfectly normal having these scoundrels as allies, for my father had associated with the same type of people when he was younger. By sixteen, I was drinking, gambling, smoking and hanging out with a gang. I began stealing liquor from my parents' store and would often share it with my friends.

The first pistol I ever owned was pawned to me by a senior member of the same gang. I thought of the gun as an accessory more than anything else. I started bringing it to school in my schoolbag, along with a bottle of liquor, so that I could show my friends how bad and *cheng* (cool) I was. I began associating being a 'good boy' with boredom. Adolescence is undoubtedly a time for finding one's sense of self and for rebelling against authority figures, but I took it too far. I started showing up at school drunk and reeking of alcohol. My attitude screamed loudly that I no longer cared about the place . . . or very much else for that matter. Teachers occasionally asked to see me after class to tentatively enquire after my well-being and whether I was experiencing problems at home. I revelled in the idea of being a problematic student—I wore this label as a badge of honour and loved being the centre of attention.

I drank so heavily that my face became bloated and I started to neglect my appearance. There were times I was too drunk to care enough to shower. I began to skip school which caused my grades to nosedive, and I lied to my parents that my schoolwork was as good as always; sadly, they took my word for it.

Wherever I went I was armed with a bottle of booze. Girls were attracted to the bad-boy image; but ironically, despite the charisma I projected, I was still too shy to make the first move, restrained by a combination of fear and pride. I was terrified I might perform poorly in bed revealing just how inexperienced I really was.

Fortunately, by the time my alcohol addiction had become fully fledged, I simply didn't have enough room in my life for other dependencies. My friends offered me a variety of drugs, which I always tried for fear of being called a sissy. I sampled marijuana and sniffed glue during my final year of secondary level. Marijuana made me smile and laugh a lot but that was about it; after its effects wore off, I never craved it as I did liquor. Sniffing glue didn't really appeal to me either; I used amphetamines on and off but I found the effects torturous—they kept me awake half the night and I couldn't sit still for longer than a few seconds at a time. Alcohol was therefore my first choice.

I soon became known as one of the biggest troublemakers in my village. I would pick fights with anyone who gave me a disapproving glance. If someone crossed me, I spitefully ordered a member of my gang to slug him.

My parents grew increasingly concerned. My mother despairingly said she wanted her old son back; conversely, my father advised me that if I was going to be bad then I might as well be terrible. He wanted me to pursue an honest path in life but, as he said, 'You're on the back of a tiger now. There's no point in getting off or it'll eat you.' I think he meant that through my actions I'd already made a lot of enemies; it was too late now to do a U-turn and become a better person—there would be too many scores to settle.

In retrospect, I underestimated my parents concerns.

CHAPTER 3

I can only lament as I recall those times. When I ran out of money, I stealthily snuck into my home like a starved dog, seeking out booze and banknotes. I quickly set to work pocketing bottles of whisky and stuffing money into my jeans before making a speedy getaway on my accomplice's motorbike. I avoided my parents and siblings, all of whom by then were gravely disappointed with me. I had alienated myself from my own people —from those nearest and dearest to me. I was a thief in my own house.

As I grew into my late teens, the neighbours gossiped about my faults and failings. I became hardened by a lack of conscience and I didn't feel nor fear their contempt. However, the real victims of this ridicule felt everything. My parents' child-rearing abilities came into question and they were deeply hurt by the harsh criticism they were affronted with. The scornful murmurs became more prevalent when my family's financial status started to deteriorate. There were huge gambling debts mounting with creditors demanding their dues. Additionally, my parents ran our grocery store poorly and neglected to use even the most basic accounting. Furthermore, my father's misguided generosity of supplying food and beer to his friends made matters even worse.

My parents hastily sold off some of their land, and took out a loan in order to repay the most urgent debts. The rest of us chipped in any way we could to maintain face within the community. Although I was selfish in the extreme, I cared about my family's reputation. There's nowhere to run in such a small village, so keeping our standing intact was of the utmost importance. My younger sister Nuan had never showed much promise at school and was the first child asked to sacrifice her education. After all, education was considered a waste of money and time for girls when they could easily be married off and taken care of by their future husbands. Over the next few years, the rest of my siblings were requested to sacrifice their schooling for the sake of the family's reputation, and in order that I might pursue higher education. At the time I simply took all this for granted.

While many factors contributed to our financial woes, I was the main cause of my family's downfall; after all I was stealing their money to throw away at gambling dens and to maintain my friends' loyalty. There is a Thai proverb that states *Tam di, dai di, tam chua, dai chua,* 'Do good or bad and you'll be rewarded accordingly.' I was soon to see just how much my behaviour would take a hold of my life and rob me of my future.

My parents sadly informed me that they couldn't afford to send me to the prestigious school in Ubon Ratchathani Province, as they'd always planned. A minority of the more fortunate children from my village were sent to this school. This was viewed as a great achievement and another way for parents to earn face. Not that I cared about study, but I'd dreamt of using such an opportunity to make my name known in Ubon. I also desired to be far from my parents in order to pursue my ruffian lifestyle freely.

I took the news very badly. I didn't hide the fact I blamed my parents for destroying my noble aspirations and I openly railed against sticking it out at the local no-name school for three more years. I chose to free-fall headlong down an even more destructive path just to spite my parents. I thus became more aggressive and violent than before.

When I came to be the *luk pi* or 'leader' of my gang I spent even less time at home and school. My favourite pastime was making grandiose entrances at local temple or makeshift fairs. My hooligan image was bolstered by the cronies sauntering obediently behind me. We liked to shoot off our mouths and flex our muscles at these celebrations, which often resulted in bloody fights with opposing gangs. Eventually my reputation preceded me and organizers, who were afraid that I was going to ruin the event, made it clear that I was not welcome.

At one such temple fair as I was dancing, a much younger boy from another gang walked straight up to me—probably in response to a dare—grabbed my collar and held his fist up ready to hit me. I stood still and stared at him, taunting him to throw the punch.

'Go ahead. What's stopping you, you little bastard?' Due to my posse looming in the background and my fearless stance, he chickened out and retreated quickly.

'I'm going to teach this sissy a lesson!' I shouted and I ran to a food cart, took a glass bottle and headed towards my assailant. The fair attendees gasped as I raced by them in hot pursuit. With a swift blow, I smashed the bottle on his head. Blood poured down his face instantly as he collapsed to the floor. I threw the remainder of the bottle at his prostrate body and marched off in a proud huff.

Once his family learnt about his public humiliation, they demanded an apology and 10,000 baht in *kha tam kwan*, compensation to help them come to terms with the situation. I adamantly refused to entertain their requests. They stated that the boy had dignity and I had no right to take that from him or them. I responded that he was the one who provoked me and I also had dignity, which I merely defended. I pointed out that my father was a teacher and my mother a renowned medium and that they were only poor farmers, so I didn't understand what the boy had to be proud of. I justified my actions because he was beneath me and therefore it was I who had been gravely insulted. His family backed downed and never bothered me again. On reflection, their attempts at recovering face and my defence of my own seems trivial and childish. Sadly, this petty victory emboldened me to believe that I could take on anyone.

Inevitably, there were plenty of folk who wanted to put me in my place. When I did go to school, I was a drunken nuisance. After hearing the teachers' complaints, a seasoned, local soldier thought he'd bring me down a peg or two. He took it upon himself to enlighten me as to what tough love meant.

I was blithely drinking in the schoolyard when he marched over to me and slapped my face indignantly. 'What utter rubbish you are! Pull yourself together!' he barked inches from my face. I was shocked but managed to shoot back an angry look before he slapped and punched me repetitively until my nose bled. My face was numb, and my ears rang—I feared I'd become deaf. Some schoolmates looked on in complete disbelief, having moved a safe distance away. These dared not interfere; meanwhile others obviously took pleasure in my utter humiliation. Undoubtedly, they thought it served me right to be attacked in such a manner. As I came to my senses, I turned red with fury, I could feel my indignation rising, ready to explode. As soon as he turned his back on me, I lunged forward, grabbed him in a headlock and began punching at his muscular body. He was almost twice my size and shook me off easily, and wailed into me some more. All I could do was to wriggle out of his grip and run for my life before he inflicted serious damage. It was my first taste of being reined in, but I didn't learn my lesson. If anything, it fully reinforced my resentment of those in charge.

On another occasion my cousin and I spent the evening at a busy fair. This was comprised of makeshift shops, amusement rides, games, a boxing ring and an outdoor cinema. I was already flying from one too many drinks, while my cousin was at least sober enough to talk reasonably. Eventually, he wanted to call it a night but I desired to continue carousing and insisted he stay. A fight quickly erupted. We wrestled, yelled obscenities at each other and made a grand disturbance. I chased him around playfully but it must have looked as if I was bullying him.

Suddenly, I felt a heavy blow to my stomach which sucked the air out of me and caused my legs to collapse. A group of men, led by the village chief, grabbed my arms and dragged me to a deserted field nearby. It was dark except for the ominous circles of light emanating from their handheld lamps. Apparently, it was the fair organisers' complaints about me that prompted this response. A lamp was held to my face as one of them yelled, 'Who the hell do you think you are to disturb others' fun, huh?' I observed that they'd encircled me and were armed with thick planks. They were more than ready to beat the living daylights out of me; in fact they looked as if they'd relish it. My tough guy persona dissolved as I knelt shivering like a newly hatched bird. It might sound strange to you but this was the village chief's method of keeping peace. Thais call this local justice *san tia*, that is, taking matters to the lower court. This was the way goons were taught their lesson, although sometimes things got too heavy-handed.

'Let's beat the bastard to a pulp, sir!' one of the vigilantes shouted as he menacingly pointed a board to my head looking to the village chief for approval. Fortunately, my victim's relative had seen them drag me off and came running to my rescue. He begged them to spare me and deliberately dropped my father's name as he pleaded for mercy. The chief narrowed his eyes angrily, then reluctantly told his men to release me. He squatted down, looked into my eyes, and poked my forehead with force. 'Worthless waste of life that you are, I'll let you go this time. I'm well acquainted with your old man and he's all right. Don't let me see you around here again, or else . . .'

I have no doubts that they would've savagely beaten, or even killed me if it hadn't been for the good deeds my father performed for the village. Good deeds or not, the villagers would have thought the chief had done them a favour by eradicating another troublemaker. It was a close call!

The first thing that came to mind after my fear subsided was my father's words. I couldn't as yet come down from the back of the tiger as there were still other people who wanted me dead. Standing alone I most likely would not survive.

One last incident that helped drive this point home happened when, as usual, I was drunk. I happened upon the village inspector—a local sheriff—named Chit. I held a deep-seated grudge against him for I perceived he'd been acting aloofly towards me. He used to be one of my many drinking buddies before being elected to his new position. Suddenly he had become too good to drink with the likes of me. So I sent out a challenging insult.

'Chit you pompous snob!' It was ridiculous for me to call anyone else arrogant, but in my conceit I did. My pride directed my temper and my mouth followed suit.

'Look who stoops to grace us with his presence. Do you also expect us to bow to you, oh mighty toad? Was it not recently you who came begging my parents for their votes? You wouldn't have your position if it weren't for the likes of us.' My friends cheered and let out peals of laughter as they applauded my rebukes. I threw down my final challenge 'Come on. I can take you out with a single punch!'

Almost as soon as these words rang out, all laughter ceased. Chit pulled out his pistol and aimed it at me. While I carried a gun, sometimes it wasn't loaded; this was one of those times. So I did the only thing I could, I ran for my life. Chit pursued, propelled by rage, threatening me with all sorts of retribution once he caught me. I flew into the sanctuary of my home and hid behind my father who was stationed in the doorway. He quickly realised what was about to ensue and begged Chit for mercy. My parents pleaded and reasoned that he shouldn't have taken offence at the words of a drunken, stupid man. He eventually conceded and walked away after much grovelling and pleading on my parents' part. I could only cower behind their backs. I had dragged my parents into a dangerous arena because of my mischief and put them at serious risk by forcing them to protect me. Shame engulfed me as I reflected on my parents' love and willingness to do anything to safeguard me, their ungrateful son, even to the point of standing in the way of a possible gunshot.

That was the last straw. I realised there would always be someone bigger and meaner out there who would be ready to take me out. I couldn't stay on top forever. I concluded that my drinking buddies could easily become my enemies one day. All it would take was a small misguided tilt of a whiskey glass or a misunderstood word. There was no shortage of gunmen for hire in my tiny lawless world. I'd erroneously thought I had been working my way up the ladder of power while, in reality, I was digging myself deeper into a hole. This hole looked like a game at first, but as the stakes got higher, I knew I could never win. I had to stop playing for good.

I was too afraid to face the person I'd become or to ask for help. Instead I poured drink down my throat, temporarily sending my mistakes into exile through merrymaking. Even though I was drunk most of the time, I managed to keep my head down over the following months and avoided trouble in order to finish high school.

I barely made it through. I failed in English and physics because I didn't complete the specified assignments. I was granted an additional month to work on the AWOL assignments in order to finally pass. In the meantime, other students were preparing for the national entrance exam to compete for a place at university. I'd lost the drive to participate in the upcoming tests.

My days continued in the same negative fashion for the following year; the only difference was I was not out challenging others to fight. My father had had enough of my purposelessness and instructed me to look to my uncle Mana as an example. Pa told me that his little brother left Sisaket to find work in the seaside tourist town of Pattaya and had been doing exceedingly well. Uncle Mana didn't ask for monetary help from anyone to start his venture, in fact he sent money back to his parents every month to help support them. As a Thai, I knew all too well that this was expected of a child—to show gratitude to his parents for giving him life by supporting them in their later years. Pa insisted that I should ask Mana for help to find a job in Pattaya. I'm sure he hoped I'd also send him and Mae support. With an ever growing record of embarrassing failures and with my list of enemies growing, I decided to flee to the safety of Pattaya and start my life anew.

After a long bus journey, I arrived at what seemed to be a brightly lit world of fun and pleasure. I was exhausted yet highly surprised. It was as if I had stepped into a red-light funfair with streets full of fancy hotels, exotic foreigners, and sophisticated women, and a nightlife that made Pattaya a far cry from my rural village.

During our first meeting, Uncle Mana reminisced about his early days in Pattaya as a poolside waiter for a hotel. He worked for a very low wage but got ample tips. He'd worked hard, slowly climbing the hotel career ladder, before becoming a manager of a small hotel. Mana made no bones over the fact that he knew of my past; he solemnly told me he believed that I could turn my life around if I took advantage of this new environment and the chance I was being given. Uncle Mana freely offered not only his advice but also his hospitality, allowing me to stay with him in his home.

My first real job was as a cleaner at Mana's hotel. It had a popular discotheque which was frequented by Thais and foreigners alike. Part of my job description was to clean the toilets. I was disgusted. As others were having fun, I was forced to clean up their mess and vomit. I felt especially humiliated working in the presence of female patrons; I worried what they must have thought of me—a lowly cleaning boy. My uncle was trying to teach me a lesson; however, I was insulted. After all, he practically ran the hotel and the best he could give his nephew was a cleaning job. I endured it for a few months before I started to look for something better.

CHAPTER 4

While seeking a job elsewhere as a waiter, I began practising English with hotel patrons. My interest in the language was piqued when a *farang* tipped me 30 baht simply for pressing the elevator button for him. My instant impression of *farangs* was that they were rich and extremely generous, so I started making a conscious effort to converse with them in the hope that my endeavours would be rewarded.

After my English skills improved, I applied for a job at an upscale restaurant. The interviewer tested me on my ability to pronounce basic greetings in English— the good-morning-and-how-are-you kind of thing. They also tested me on laying tables and on the correct manner to serve customers. Thanks to my uncle and the stint I'd done in his hotel, I was well prepared for the interview and got the job.

I found working as a waiter fairly pleasant, and it was definitely far more dignified than cleaning toilets. My wage was 1,100 baht a month but I could easily make about 200-300 baht extra each day in tips. These wages were considered very reasonable, especially since I didn't have to pay rent and split the electricity and water bills with my uncle. In fact, I could have lived quite comfortably on my tips alone. I was delighted, and felt that I was finally beginning to find my footing. I was earning good money for doing a relatively easy job—I didn't have to sweat under the hot sun like the poor labourers who slaved away at constructing the luxury high-rise buildings that dotted the coastline.

Unfortunately, my newfound self-esteem morphed into reckless arrogance. Working in the restaurant gave me access to large stocks of foreign cigarettes and alcohol. I'd been used to *lao khao*, *Mae Khong* whiskey, and *Krong Thip* cigarettes, which were, in my estimation, poor imitations of these luxurious Western goods. No longer wanting to appear as an unsophisticated country boy, I opted for expensive opulent brands. Dunhill and Winston were my favourite smokes. I assumed these status symbols helped establish me as a manly man.

After five or six months of working in the restaurant, I got fired. I was in the habit of going to clubs after work and would show up the next day sleepy and hung-over. On nights when tips were particularly high, I'd disappear with my buddies for a few days straight and squander everything in nightclubs and gambling houses. I also had anger issues which would flare up easily if a co-worker made complaints about me to my boss. So I began threatening the staff with violence for what I saw as betrayal. I was convinced they were jealous that my English was better than theirs, and therefore, that I was getting more tips as a result. One evening, my manager had enough and called me into his office, sacking me on the spot. Sadly, this wasn't an isolated incident and history was to repeat itself several times over. I usually managed to walk into jobs with ease and became overly confident in my abilities. I was adept at making a good first impression but generally neglected to maintain it.

While job-hopping, I was often approached by hotel guests asking me to procure marijuana for them. Of course, I knew exactly who to go to. As luck would have it, the neighbours in my *soi* happened to be small-time dealers. After securing a deal, I'd hide the goods under my serving platter and discreetly pass it onto buyers. I paid the dealers 50-100 baht for marijuana and then resold it at ten times the price; it was a lucrative setup. I didn't even think twice about the trouble I could get into if I got caught. I offered to take charge of room service whenever possible because, not only were the tips better, but also, there was a greater chance of meeting potential drug buyers. I filled in as a bellboy whenever the need arose, and for exactly the same reason.

The extra cash allowed me to develop an expensive lifestyle that I found difficult to maintain. When I had money I spent it; I never managed to save, let alone send much home to my parents. I squandered it all on fine dining, gambling, beer, prostitutes, and dance clubs. Pattaya was full of delights and I depleted my resources faster than I ever did in Sisaket. My life was like a rollercoaster; I would start the evening with a full wallet, have a good time, and come home completely broke. Thrift was an alien concept to me. Growing up,

I was never taught to be frugal and so I didn't see the need for it; besides, life was too much fun.

The only thing that remained the same from one job to another was my work ethic and my extravagance. At one job, I 'borrowed' a keg of beer from the storeroom and generously shared it with my co-workers. When the supervisor realised the keg was missing, he began an investigation. One by one, my drinking accomplices pointed the finger of blame in my direction. I assured my supervisor that I'd cover all expenses with my next pay packet but he didn't want to hear of it. I cursed my co-workers and quit before the supervisor could fire me.

Besides all the drinking and gambling during this time, there were the women. I fell for a lovely waitress named Pat who hailed from Pichit Province. Whenever the opportunity presented itself, I'd walk her home after work. I made sure she knew my intentions were noble and I wouldn't take advantage of her. It was likely she considered me a potential beau because my uncle was a hotel manager. Whether or not this was the case, being his nephew certainly did me no harm when it came to the ladies.

I desperately wanted to consummate my relationship with Pat but there was one problem—I didn't know how to make the first move. I was afraid that if I merely took her hand in mine, she'd consider me lecherous. The only time we shared physical contact was during a particularly bumpy tuk-tuk ride when we jolted up against the other. It would have been highly immodest of Pat to initiate any sexual intimacy. However, she seemed to be allowing the jolts to throw us together. I interpreted this as her way of intimating that she wanted me to make a move, only I was too shy to do so. Pat took my lack of initiative as a sign of weakness and said she no longer wanted my company. Less than a week later, I saw her walking arm in arm with another man.

I had viewed Pat as a conservative girl and wanted to get to know her properly before moving on to the next level. I had put her on a pedestal that she didn't want to be on. My friend laughed at my predicament, telling me that it was no one's fault but my own for not consummating the relationship. He haughtily informed me that the only way to cement things with a woman was to strike her with one's sword as quickly as possible. I was still green when it came to relationships; it wasn't until I had ample practice with prostitutes that I mastered the art of bedding women.

I confided to my friend that, at nearly 20 years of age, I'd never slept with a woman and I desperately wanted to try it out. To remedy my malady, he immediately brought me to a hotel which was aptly named '69 Hotel'. On the surface it looked like a run-of-the-mill flophouse. My friend, a regular at such places, was familiar with the protocol. When we entered the hotel coffee shop, I noticed twenty girls lounging about, chatting and preening themselves while giving sidelong glances to any man who happened to stroll in. In my innocence, I thought they were friends hanging out together in a hotel. If I hadn't been told they could be purchased I'd have been none the wiser. I finally mustered the courage to negotiate the price with a pimp who informed me I could take my pick of the beauties available and, if I remember correctly, it cost 200 baht to have a quickie with the younger ones. This fee was reduced for the older women who were well worn by the trade. Most of the girls came from the north of Thailand: *sao nuea*, or 'northern girls', generally have a fair complexion and demure appearance. One of the girls was sitting quietly in the corner and I was immediately drawn to her. Her long black hair framed her beautiful oval face. I decided she was the one for me and in no time we disappeared into an upstairs room. When we were alone, like a true veteran, she sensed my anxiety.

'Are you shy?' she asked.

'It's . . . it's my first time,' I replied.

Her sensitivity disappeared momentarily and she burst out laughing.

'Where have you been all these years?'

The sight of my face turning crimson with embarrassment made her compose herself. She patted the bed to indicate I should take a seat. I was shorter than her and this made me feel very self-conscious.

'Why don't you take off your clothes,' she said.

'Can you turn off the light first?'

I didn't want her to see my already erect member.

'Don't be nervous.' She reassured me. 'There's a first time for everything. My name is Ple and I'll be your teacher tonight and teach you how to please a woman.'

My shyness quickly vanished. It felt completely right sleeping with Ple; the sensation of touching, tasting, and being a part of a woman was incredible. Before I left the room, she smiled at me and softly crooned that I should come back to visit her again soon.

From that day on, I found it impossible to concentrate on my work; all I could think about was Ple. Surprisingly, I found myself working harder than ever; desperately wanting to earn enough money to be able to see her. Each time I did so, I excitedly made my way to the hotel to act out my passions. I fell for her and was convinced my feelings would be reciprocated. Finally, I bared my heart, asking Ple to be my girl.

I couldn't believe it when she declined, 'You're infatuated with me. Well, not exactly me but the sex haze you're caught up in. It isn't love that you're experiencing. And, frankly, you're just a client to me.'

After Ple broke my heart, I indulged in different working girls. I regarded this as one of the most importance aspects of life in Pattaya. I also adjusted my thinking—there were plenty of other Ple's out there so why limit myself to just one?

One day I turned up for my shift at the coffee shop in a terrible state. A *farang* gentleman Chris, who was a regular customer, called in for a drink. He was nice and we'd had a few chats before. On this particular day,

I was depressed and badly needed to talk to someone about my constant shortage of money. Chris walked in as if on cue. I found *farangs* in general to be relaxed and less easily offended than Thais. More importantly, they didn't consider it beneath them to talk to a waiter, unlike my fellow countrymen. In my best English and with as much courage as I could muster, I poured out my unhappiness and discouragement at not being able to meet my expenses. Chris listened attentively, giving reassuring smiles and sympathetic nods at appropriate intervals. I then asked if he was willing to take me out for a few drinks—at his own expense naturally—to help me forget my problems. In return, I assured him I'd show him around town as his guide. He looked a little taken aback by my bluntness but eventually agreed. I would never be so brazen with any of my Thai compatriots let alone a customer. Imagine requesting free drinks with a side order of sympathy?

Chris and I hit several places in South Pattaya, including a go-go bar where I feasted my eyes on the luscious bodies of beautiful, scantily clad girls. Smug in my new-found friendship with Chris, I thought to myself how easy it was to befriend a *farang*.

In the small hours of the morning, I took him to my uncle's house to show him off to the neighbours as one would a trophy. I knew I would earn kudos by flaunting my *farang* friend and especially for the fact that I was able to converse with him in English. A group of neighbours congregated on our porch drinking and shooting the breeze merrily, while my prize white man hovered in the background. Chris and I went into the house to use the bathroom. As we climbed the stairs, he asked to see my room and I drunkenly obliged. The next thing I remember was Chris fondling my penis eagerly. One thing led to another, and he pulled down my pants and began to pleasure me with his mouth. It was like a flashback from the experiences with my teacher five years before. My well-practised ability to draw pleasure without acknowledging the source kicked in. This prevented me from experiencing revulsion at what was transpiring. The main difference between Chris and my teacher was that Chris was more polite and gentle, and he took the time to arouse me.

Before we parted ways, Chris handed me 1,000 baht. My feelings of delight completely quelled any twinges of guilt. I simply reassured myself by saying, '*Mai pen rai*,' 'Never mind, it's not a big deal.' I had a good time and had been well paid and that was all that mattered. Chris dressed and left the house before I returned downstairs to join my drinking neighbours. They easily guessed at what had just taken place and couldn't wait to tease me mercilessly.

'Chai, we didn't know that you like boys now.'

I wondered how they'd figured it out because Chris looked like any other straight man in his late forties. He sported a pencil-thin moustache and handsome grey sideburns, which flatteringly accentuated his dark slicked-back hair. He was as dashing as Errol Flynn. In his polo shirt, pressed trousers, and expensive leather shoes, women should have been queuing up for him.

When I offered to be his impromptu guide, I didn't expect the sale of my body would be part of the package. As for my uncle, he couldn't believe that after all these months in Pattaya, I still hadn't been able to tell Chris was gay.

He joined in the teasing, 'Ati, which is Chinese for 'boy', you must now be gay because you let that *farang* blow your flute!'

I felt ashamed and my silent response ignited even more roars of laughter.

'Don't worry. It was business. I won't tell your Pa.'

The fact that my uncle and neighbours openly joked without malice about what had just transpired made it all seem somehow above board. After all, I was only doing it for money—*mai pen rai*.

From that day on, each evening Chris would wait for me to finish up in the coffee shop. We both knew the score and followed it religiously. Chris would wine and dine me, perform oral sex, and then pay me handsomely in return. How could I refuse such a deal? His sexual orientation aside, Chris was very different from the other men I'd met. He was highly civil and seemed blind to my many flaws. He adored the fact that I was short, which was almost too good to be true; while I was attracted to his easy-going, fun-loving nature. He appeared to be happily cruising through life without attracting any trouble. While I certainly knew how to have fun, I would inevitably end up in some kind of disaster or other.

Later on, when my friends made fun of my relationship with Chris, I made light of the situation by claiming that I was uniquely gifted in having the ability to bat for both teams.

Although I enjoyed Chris's affections, I essentially thought of him as an ATM—something that magically dispensed money whenever I needed it. Additionally, Chris was good company and I enjoyed being seen with a smart-looking *farang*. I fantasised about how much easier life would be if I was genuinely attracted to him. We could easily live happily ever after, and I'd never have to work again.

As our relationship progressed, I began to reciprocate Chris's affections, and began caressing and touching his body as he did mine. My motives were purely self-serving however, and didn't stem from genuine passion as Chris would have liked to believe. I wanted to make sure he wouldn't lose interest in me. I never did anything more than touch and cuddle him though. When he tried to kiss me on the mouth I'd wriggle free of his embrace. I allowed him to caress my face and body but the idea of engaging in full-blown man-on-man acts made me freeze up.

If you'd asked me if I considered myself a prostitute, the answer would have been a resounding 'No!' After all, I didn't dance in a go-go bar or walk the streets. Looking back, I now know what prostitution is regardless of how one solicits the customer.

On the last day of Chris's stay in Thailand, he gave me his address. He asked me to write and promised to send me a monthly allowance. I felt I'd hit the jackpot, 10,000 to 20,000 baht in exchange for a few letters would be splendid. Unfortunately, as fate, or rather my stupidity, would have it, I lost Chris's card during an outrageously drunken night on the town. I still kick myself when I think how foolish I was to lose his address. His money would have secured me a good future. I was certainly neither Chris's first dependent nor would I be his last; experience has taught me that these kinds of relationships never last. It would only have been a matter of time before someone else replaced me in Chris's heart and I hope, for Chris's sake, that it was someone who loved him.

Chris was the first gay man who treated me with dignity. I hadn't a clue about the gay scene even though it was clearly thriving in the place I resided. I had several Pattaya friends who became go-go boys after losing big in gambling houses; I was continuously amazed at the amount of money they had and the ease with which they made it. They could lose huge sums one night only to return the following evening full of zeal and with their fortunes replenished. Unlike today, there were only a few go-go bars in Pattaya at the time. During one of my many periods of unemployment, I befriended several go-go boys who asked me to work a scam by helping them steal money from their clients in hotel rooms. Many of these tricksters were actually straight and would pair up with working girls to operate as a team. The more I hung around with go-go boys and listened to them brag about their wealth, the more I considered becoming one. On the surface, they were the picture of respectability—they dressed well, ate at nice places, and seemed to have bottomless wallets. I'd never been in a male go-go bar and had no understanding of how they operated. Therefore, I had certain reservations about joining their ranks.

I eventually decided to leave Pattaya altogether; I was done with the city. I didn't make a fortune like my father had hoped, and I wouldn't be returning home a hero. I rarely sent money to my parents and the total sum of my contribution was mere pittance in comparison with the amount I'd blown. I was still the drunkard gambler I'd always been. The only lesson I'd learned from my stay in Pattaya was that I knew, without doubt, I didn't want to work long, boring hours, day after day, in order to collect miniscule wages from what I considered to be snooty bosses.

During the long restless bus ride back to Sisaket, I found my thoughts continually returning to the idea of becoming a go-go boy. I already had some experience at sleeping with men for money and I reasoned that such a life could provide me with an escape route to a brighter future. My greed seemed to override any rational or moral consideration. I'd made approximately 1,000 baht a month working as a waiter; a go-go boy could earn at least the same amount in a day. I concluded that the insanity lay in not becoming one. I knew I'd have to participate in some disagreeable activities, just like when I gave my body to my teacher and Chris; but

it'd be nothing in comparison to the humiliating and
unrewarding work of a waiter or cleaner.

With each passing kilometre on the way to Sisaket,
I felt these thoughts beginning to take root in my heart
and mind.

CHAPTER 5

Upon arriving home, my parents greeted me with huge smiles. The fact that I'd managed to support myself in Pattaya for the last two years led them to expect the return of a new-and-improved Chai. Of course, they didn't know about my appalling work ethic, or the fact that I'd been fired from countless jobs; nor the kind of people I regularly associated with, most of them not impartial to gambling, drinking and prostitution. Not that I was innocent of these vices myself.

My parents thanked me for the pitifully infrequent sums of money I'd sent them. This money hadn't even made a dent in the total debt of hundreds of thousands of baht they owed. I felt dreadful. In their desire to see the good in me, they overrated my achievements, and stubbornly clung to the belief that their formerly dutiful son was still lurking somewhere inside of me.

Our large home was eerily empty for my siblings had been forced to leave Sisaket in search of work in other provinces. The grocery store was equally bare as all our former customers had turned their backs on us.

I slowly began to re-adjust myself to rural life, and sought out childhood friends. I was confident I'd be well received but I was in for a shock. Sirin, my first girlfriend, who'd walked away when my delinquent nature proved too much, still wanted nothing to do with me. I learned from others that she was pursuing her lifelong ambition of becoming a nurse. My male friends, who were in their sophomore year at university, working towards future careers in the civil service, also distanced themselves from me. A gulf divided us; we lived in different worlds—theirs being far superior to mine. A sense of self-pity combined with jealousy clouded my mind, and true to form, I found comfort and escape in alcohol. The more aware I was of what a wasteland my future seemed to be, the more consumed with self-hatred I became. How many other people my age, having their whole lives ahead of them, could so assuredly pronounce that they despised the person they'd become?

I was no longer on a mission to find trouble, yet trouble still managed to find me. It wasn't as if anyone else would keep me company, so it was hard to shun the sort that were associated with alcohol. In a preemptive strike, my parents offered to support me through university. They were already deeply in debt and couldn't afford this additional expense, but were desperate to save me and preserve the tiny shred of dignity our family had left. In hindsight, I accepted their offer with only a vague intention of reforming. I'd been away from books so long that the prospect of returning to academia seemed surreal. With no other option, I wearily surrendered to my parents' wishes.

I didn't study much for the entrance exam for the faculty of humanities at Rajabhat University in Ubon Ratchathani. Considering I'd developed some English skills, it made sense to improve them further academically. My nonchalant attitude didn't leave me holding very high hopes of passing the exam, but surprisingly, I got the grades and was accepted into the course. However, since my score was unremarkable, I was sent to study at a less prestigious campus in Kampeangphet Province towards the northern region of Thailand. My parents were nonetheless delighted; Pa patted me on the back, joking that some sort of divine intervention must have caused me to pass since my brain surprisingly still functioned despite all the alcohol I'd consumed.

On orientation day, while I was waiting to enter the auditorium for the dean's welcoming speech, I noticed that female students outnumbered males by a three-to-one ratio. I took note that the female dormitory was located next to the auditorium. Groups of girls, wearing short skirts and tight blouses, were huddled together, nervously chatting away. Maybe university wouldn't be so bad after all.

I was like a rooster in a henhouse and, in order to attract the resident chicks, I knew that I'd need to stock up on both cigarettes and booze. Once again, the old me was making a hearty comeback. In no time, I drank beer and smoked in deliberate bad-boy style, whilst relishing the disapproving looks I attracted from other students. Such behaviour was forbidden on campus, and their reactions served only to egg me on. Unlike the bright-eyed freshmen, I was not excited at the prospect of pursuing a higher education and I made no secret of this fact. I was certainly entrepreneurial enough to cash in on any opportunities that came my way though—especially ones wrapped in short skirts.

While I continued to theatrically hone my persona, I still managed to absorb some studies, only barely scraping by. But I did make some friends and was reasonably popular.

I bragged to peers about my work experience in Pattaya as a 'tour guide'. In the presence of other students, I chatted merrily away with the only American teacher in my faculty. I wanted them to think I was brave and intelligent for being able to converse with a Westerner. In reality, many of the students probably knew more vocabulary and had a better understanding of grammar than I did, but were afraid to approach the teacher lest they make a mistake and appear stupid.

I deliberately unbuttoned the collar of my shirt allowing other students to see an expensive necklace I'd bought with some lottery winnings. I regularly purchased such tickets but rarely won; however, a recent windfall ensured that I could afford such an impressive-looking ornament. While the necklace certainly boosted my appeal among the girls, it was also a nest egg that would be sold at a later date if I needed cash.

Due to its size, I had a hard time convincing my friends that it was real. When I offhandedly confided with my parents about my friends' doubts, my father got angry. He took it personally believing he'd lost face. Pa managed to wrangle another loan from a welfare programme and put a deposit on a pick-up truck for me. This was an expensive way of making a fool out of my classmates for doubting our wealth. In reality, my classmates probably didn't mean to insult us; they simply teased me good-humouredly as Thais love to do. I should have refused to allow my father to plunge the family further into debt, but once again willpower failed me. While my father was enslaved by his preoccupation with saving face, I was in bondage to my oversized ego. Within a week, I was driving to campus in a white-elephant pick-up truck.

With the benefit of hindsight, I now understand my father's reasoning. He evaluated his success as a father by his ability to provide for me. He strove to satisfy every need and desire, however misguided, in an attempt to be the best father he could be. Now that I'm a father and rice-winner myself, I understand how difficult it was for Pa. I find it nearly impossible to refuse my son's requests, no matter how unnecessary they may be. I often find myself over-indulging him to compensate for the trauma I've caused him during his young life.

It wasn't long before I made enemies at university with a gang of male seniors who took offence at my cockiness. I was oblivious to their resentment until a neighbouring student alerted me that they'd come banging on my door while I was out. Trouble was brewing and I knew I had to find some protection quickly.

I set my sights on befriending Den who was one of the most influential young men in the province. He happened to be the eldest son of a well-known village chief and headed a gang of five *luk nongs*, or 'subordinates'. I met him during a visit to a gambling house and we immediately bonded due to our shared passion of leading destructive lifestyles. My bravery therefore began to increase as a result of this unholy alliance. Although it was fear that initially drove me into Den's arms, I soon found myself comforted by the gang's communality; after all, I knew the gangster way of life like the back of my hand.

I decided it was time to settle scores with the seniors so Den, his men and I decided to confront them. On the day of reckoning, hostilities began with a lot of cursing, yelling and threatening; but this would soon escalate into a full-fledged fistfight. There was no contest between the two gangs and we easily emerged as victors. As they lay scattered on the ground, nursing their injuries, I drew my pistol and pointed it at them in order to remind them who was boss. The sight of the pistol terrified them. As we ordered our hostages to huddle together on the ground, they instinctively joined their hands together in the prayer-like *wai* position, stuttering as they begged us to spare them. Their pathetic tears had the effect of calming me down as I realised how ludicrous the situation was—I was frightening them to within an inch of their lives with an unloaded pistol. I walked away while Den called me a chicken for not delivering at least a few more blows.

One day, I staggered drunk and barefoot to the house of a girl I was seeing. Rin was an attractive, naïve, first-year student from another faculty and we were an odd couple. I'd grown my hair long by then to further enhance my ruffian looks. The scruffier I appeared the better—I wore dirty shirts and slacks and went days at a time without a shower; I looked like a derelict.

I was feeling particularly horny and my libido was angrily demanding satisfaction. In my inebriated state I believed Rin would kindly agree to have sex with me. Of course, I failed to consider how my dirty, dishevelled appearance might prevent this from actually happening. I made my way towards her family's simple rented house near the campus. I approached the front gate and began calling her name at the top of my lungs. When she didn't come running, I climbed the fence into the yard and gathered up stones to throw at the windows. Although drunk, I still had good aim and the sound of tinkling glass joined my incessant roaring. I don't remember anything else after that as I then passed out.

When I finally came to, the world was spinning in a blur of varying colours. The merry-go-round gradually slowed and I became acutely aware of a gun hovering in my sideline vision. Someone was pressing it to my right temple; this shocking revelation sobered me up instantly. Thoughts scurried round my head like fervent ants.

A surly police officer, the gun's owner, gruffly shouted, 'What's a drunken burglar like you doing trying to break into the professor's house?'

I was in a police station. I struggled to respond—gasping for air only to dry-retch. It was imperative, however, that I deny these false accusations.

'Officer, I don't know what you're talking about. I was out drinking and enjoying myself. I wasn't robbing anyone—let alone a professor. Besides, I'm not a burglar; I'm a student at the university where he teaches. I thought it was my girlfriend's house.'

Given the circumstances and my dishevelled appearance, my claim of innocence fell on deaf ears. The officer grew increasingly irritated and offered not an ounce of sympathy. He began pummelling me with his fists and boots, paying particular attention to my face and ribs. Any lingering trace of drunkenness vanished—although this was the one time being liquored up to my eyeballs would have actually served me well. No matter how guilty I looked, I certainly didn't deserve this type of treatment. He made horrible threats, assuring me that it was only a matter of time before he made me confess to the crime he knew I'd committed. He had no concrete evidence but was determined to make my case stick.

No wonder the Thai police have a less-than-favourable image where the public are concerned—parents even caution their children against misbehaviour by threatening that the big police bogeyman will get them. There have been countless cases of police brutality in

Thailand but only a paltry few have ever made the news. The police are notorious for using torture as a means of persuading people to give information. Personally, I think the most frightening example of this kind of 'persuasion' is the police's use of electrodes, which are hooked up to the scrotum and nipples of the victim while he's made to stand in a trough of water. I've heard horrible stories of people having bottles forced into their rectum during questioning; or of others being made to sit on huge blocks of ice for hours on end. On top of this, they are systematically beaten and/or raped by fellow cellmates, often at the police's own behest.

A recent scandal involved a gang of 13 border-patrol policemen who allegedly broke into the homes of innocent civilians, kidnapped them, and extorted their money and valuables. After torturing them into a confession they then falsely charged them with possession of narcotics. Such confessions could easily result in a life sentence or worse. After the gang of 13 had been arrested and placed in remand to await trial, numerous prisoners came forward. They claimed they had also been victimised and unfairly incarcerated at the hands of this gang. It makes one wonder how judges can turn a blind eye to cases that are full of glaring inconsistencies and where the police are the only witnesses.

If I compare myself to some victims, I was lucky—all I got was an old-fashioned beating. The incident once more served to intensify my contempt for authority figures. It would be many years before I met good, honest policemen who persuaded me that there are all types of people in every walk of life.

As he continued to bombard me with abusive accusations, I managed to dig deep within myself and find an inner strength I never knew I possessed. I simply refused to confess to the crimes of which I was being accused. Once my accuser tired himself out, he threw me into a cell. He was confident I was a small-time crook until a background check disclosed I was indeed a student. Despite this, he still charged me with attempted burglary.

I was kept in the cell for seven days, during which time I was permitted occasional phone calls to my parents. My first night of incarceration was one of the most traumatic experiences of my life. The beating I received began to take its toll on my body for it ballooned and began to change colour rapidly. But this pain was nothing in comparison with the overwhelming feelings of guilt that gnawed at my insides. I had disappointed my parents yet again, and I was terrified that they wouldn't believe I was innocent. After all, it wasn't as if I had a clean record.

When they eventually came to visit me, I poured out my version of events. Judging from their reaction, they seemed to believe me. Pa gritted his teeth saying very little; he seemed to be searching for the right response but was coming up blank. Mae was crying uncontrollably and almost fainted a few times from the emotional strain. She kept repeating, 'What bad karma he must have committed,' as if hoping that by openly recognising my misdeeds, a higher power might magically remove me from this tangle. I grew angry with my mother's tears—she was making a fool of me in front of the other cellmates, but worse than this, they were making me immensely sad because I knew I was to blame and I was helpless to do anything about it. Pa realised that Mae was only making a hard situation even more difficult and instructed her to compose herself. Before they left, Pa assured me that he'd do everything in his power to help me.

I later learned that the house I'd unlawfully entered was indeed not my girlfriend's. After hearing the commotion, the furious *ajarn* discovered me lying unconscious in his compound and phoned the police. Lying there, I couldn't have looked too much of a threat but I think the professor's pride was hurt and he wanted to teach me a lesson. If I hadn't spent the days prior to my arrest in a drunken stupor, things would have turned out very differently.

After a week locked in the cell, I was summoned to a preliminary hearing in the nearby provincial court, where I was remanded in custody to await my trial. During the first few days of my incarceration, I was a snivelling teary-eyed wretch. I never normally cried but the violence and harsh conditions I was subjected to on a daily basis eventually broke me; I did manage to keep such displays of emotion from the other inmates however.

One of my first initiations into prison life came when I was forced, along with the other prisoners, to witness a young inmate being brutally attacked by a team of guards and trustees. The inmate was due for release in a few months but, missing his wife, had stupidly attempted an escape. He'd been participating in a pre-release social programme that required his being sent out of prison daily to clean clogged public drains. It's filthy work, but it permits specially chosen prisoners to temporarily re-enter society and even earn some money, which they can claim when they're eventually released. This particular prisoner tried to make a run for it but other inmates had easily apprehended him at the command of the officer in charge.

He was then taken back to the prison. The guards pushed him into the prison-block backyard where he was surrounded on all sides by trustees. As they launched their attack, he fell to the ground and curled into a foetal position. He screamed for mercy as a pool of blood began spreading around him. The sounds of hard-toed boots and batons striking human flesh echoed throughout the yard. These noises amplified as the captive audience of inmates looked on in stunned silence. With each blow, we winced in horror trying not to react for fear that we might incur the same wrath. Murderers, rapists, and other hardcore criminals were all unwillingly forced to watch this horrendous demonstration. The beating served as a message to all, and it worked well as even the most hardened prisoners were reduced to trembling messes.

The inmate's moans barely sounded human—they rather resembled the sounds of a dying animal. Having myself been involved in plenty of fights didn't prepare me for such savagery. I'd never seen so much blood; it was as though they were trying to beat every last drop of it out of his body. Surprisingly, he didn't die, but was permanently maimed.

Imagine how relieved I was to find an ally on the inside—one who happened to be extremely powerful as well! He was a guard, named Niyom and our alliance came about when he casually asked me a few personal questions. His ears pricked up when he heard that I was a fellow Sisaketian. He instantly took me under his wing as he would a long-lost cousin. He read over my case and commented that the evidence against me was very weak indeed. Moreover, he was confident the court would eventually find me innocent. The problem was that it could be a very long time before they reached such a verdict. He contacted my parents, and together they came to an arrangement that would guarantee my safety while I was in prison.

I became Niyom's office boy; I cleaned and tidied his desk and made his coffee every morning. I eagerly tended to his every need no matter how trivial. In return, I was given some privileges that included being able to watch TV in his office in my spare time. I carried out these menial tasks while other prisoners were forced to work in unsafe factories or on backbreaking construction projects. Niyom's wife cooked white rice (a prison delicacy) and other tasty foods that she gave to Niyom to pass on to me and other prisoners who happened to have a similar arrangement with him. My parents also sent Niyom money regularly for snacks and desserts in order to make life a little easier for me.

Although I slept in a cell like the others, the fact that I was Niyom's boy afforded me a higher status, and nobody dared bully me. My parents visited regularly, which offered added protection as inmates and guards were aware that I still had a connection to the outside world.

If I needed evidence that it was indeed my association with Niyom that protected me, I realised it one morning when I was caught smoking by a guard. He slapped my face and then forcefully rapped his knuckles on the top of my head. As an extra punishment, he instructed me to peel off the cigarette paper and drop its tobacco into a small bowl of water. Under great duress, I was forced to drink the revolting mixture. In a moment of desperation, I squeaked out that I was Niyom's boy. He immediately snatched the bowl from me.

'Why the hell didn't you say so in the first place?' he responded in surprise.

He apologised and instructed me not to tell Niyom, who was a higher-ranking officer.

The guards earned very little, and the only thing that kept them afloat was the deals they struck with inmates and their families. Inmates desperately want to communicate with family and friends so there is a huge demand for illegal mobile phones. Such precious commodities command high rental prices amongst the inmates themselves. The daily rations of food are frequently inadequate so it's often necessary to find other sources of nourishment. Drugs can be freely purchased, and can help ease the pain, especially during long sentences. The *kha yai*, or 'heavies', use phones for drug deals, criminal arrangements, and many other scenarios outside of the prison. Considering prisoners are currently kept behind plexiglas during visits, it is completely unfeasible to import drugs or phones without the help of the guards.

Conditions inside Thai jails are so harsh it's a wonder how the justice system expects to ever rehabilitate the prisoners. I don't mean to be crude, but one of the main failings of the penal system is that it doesn't take the sexual needs of prisoners into consideration. After all, they're still human beings with the same appetites whether inside or outside a cell. If you pack so many men into confined spaces, it's inevitable that some will capitulate. It must also be taken into account that not all sexual encounters will be consensual. I overcame this by using my hand and my imagination, although this certainly wasn't easy as privacy wasn't a privilege we were entitled to. The communal bathing area tended to provide the best opportunity for meeting partners. Many long-term inmates adopted good-looking newcomers as sexual partners. These younger men were more than willing to take on the role in exchange for food and protection.

Sunday was our day off and we generally gathered in the recreational room to watch TV. However, very little

TV-viewing took place. We usually took advantage of this time to engage in intimacies with each other. Such interactions often started with playful fondling that would lead to mutual masturbation or even discreet anal sex. Meanwhile, everyone would act as if nothing was going on. I can't say I ever witnessed a prisoner being raped; what I saw were acts of survival—men who, by allowing others to use them sexually, would receive the kind of treatment in return that would ensure their safety.

Several weeks into my incarceration, I found myself looking at men in a different light. I even wondered what I'd be willing to do to find relief for my mounting sexual frustrations. But just as these temptations were starting to become appealing, my father made a call to his younger sister, the result of which changed everything. Aunt Suda worked as an assistant to a high-ranking officer in the police department in Bangkok. Her policeman husband had died on duty, leaving her three small children to raise on her own. His boss then hired her as an assistant, and in the years since, she'd worked for various other officers. My father desperately asked her to pull some strings for us. One of her bosses instructed his clerk to phone the station where I'd initially been charged to talk to the lieutenant working my case.

The lieutenant visited me in person in the holding cell during one of my court appearances. He addressed me politely in a most respectful manner, apologising for putting me in this situation. I later learned that Aunt

Suda's boss had strongly criticised him for blowing this small case out of proportion. At the time however, I was oblivious to my aunt's intervention, and was bewildered by his sudden change of heart. My parents later visited me and joyously informed me that the court would shortly be dismissing the case.

My parents were right. The judge dismissed my case and instructed that I be released on the grounds of insufficient evidence. Despite this, untold damage had been done to my family, who had spent a fortune protesting my innocence. Among the casualties of this expenditure were my necklace, which was sold, and the pick-up truck, which had to be reclaimed. In total, I spent 48 days in prison for a breaking a window. Those 48 days felt like an eternity to me.

Oddly, I found my university friends the most judgemental of all—they didn't believe for a second that I had not intended to rob the house. My parents and I agreed it would be best for me to put my education on hold. I couldn't have cared less if I never had the opportunity to resume it; I didn't want to be part of a system that, in my opinion, had betrayed me. I returned to Sisaket with my parents just as I turned 22. Yet another year under my belt, and still I'd achieved nothing.

CHAPTER 6

My failure to pursue a higher education and my imprisonment was broadcast everywhere by gossiping villagers. I decided to become a monk in order to escape the constant whispers and stares. My parents readily gave me their permission. I intended to be ordained for a three-month period, during which time I'd seek to better myself. Thai men are expected to be ordained at least twice in their lives—as a boy, and again in adulthood—in order to express gratitude to their parents by making merit on their behalf. This merit is especially important where mothers are concerned because women are forbidden to enter the monastery; therefore they can't earn merit for themselves. However, parents can cling onto their ordained child's saffron while making their ascent into heaven thus securing their own entry.

Initially I thought I would stay at a temple in my village, but this proved problematic—how could I expect anyone to respect me, let alone the robes I wore, when they knew firsthand of my grievous faults? My lengthy list of enemies could easily use my ordainment as a perfect opportunity to taunt or attack me.

I hoped to work on construction projects within a monastery because such efforts would procure greater merit. A friend recommended a simple temple in a remote part of Prachinburi Province where only a few facilities existed, so I went to survey it. There were very few monks residing in this somewhat primitive monastery and I liked it immediately. I felt I could make a real contribution there.

I'd been sober since my release from prison and this was the first time in ages I wanted to do something good, for both myself and others.

As a novice, I was ready to follow my abbot's commands. He sent me to live in an old and dirty wooden pavilion. It had only three walls, leaving one side completely open to the elements. My room was covered in cobwebs, and beneath the pavilion there were several empty coffins. There was a black *bat* on the floor, which is a bowl carried by Buddhist monks to receive offerings from the public during the morning alms. It was filled with various charms and little Buddha images that were covered in dust. I supposed it had been placed there to ward off evil and to comfort whoever occupied the room, but from the look of it, no one had taken up residence in the pavilion for years. What a foreboding place indeed. The sounds of bodhi tree branches scraping against the roof and walls as the wind blew added to the fearful atmosphere. In fact, on my first night I was so terrified, I didn't sleep a wink. I garnered some comfort from the holy robe I shrouded myself in, hoping that it might imbue me with supernatural protection against ghosts lurking in dark corners.

It was approaching dawn when I heard a sharp knocking sound. I bolted upright, trembling as I attempted to seek out its source. There was no one to be seen and I couldn't imagine what caused the noise. Then I remembered the coffins directly beneath the floor where I was sleeping. This led me to wonder just how many bodies had been held in storage awaiting cremation at this temple. I began to chant wholeheartedly as if my very life depended on it. I prayed that any good merit I'd earned thus far might be distributed to the needy spirits, and by so doing, remove their need to bother me further. I was convinced that the signal for help came from a spirit who sought a blessing that would better its status in the afterlife. From that moment on I dutifully committed to my prayers.

Not all my memories of the monastery involved fear of the supernatural however. I was entrusted with the responsibility of organising a cremation ceremony for a veteran monk who'd died 100 days before. This was a huge honour for an inexperienced novice like myself. Acts of goodness towards someone of purer status would earn one greater spiritual rewards and I was grateful to have had such an opportunity.

While being a monk was uncomplicated, it was not without its protocols. Every morning, I rose at 5am in extremely cold weather—we Thais are used to a hot climate, so when the temperature drops a few degrees we suffer. I reasoned that the more hardship I endured the greater spiritual kudos I'd earn. I walked barefoot from village to village with an assistant in tow while receiving alms from the villagers. It is customary to give food to Buddhist monks first thing in the morning; they depend on laymen for alms and basic necessities in order to lead an ascetic life and study Dhamma (the holy teachings of the Buddha). Monks in turn act as spiritual guides for those who seek answers, comfort, or even admonition.

After my morning rounds, I'd sweep up leaves, clean and trim foliage, and tend to the gardens around the temple grounds. I diligently worked at whatever form of labour was assigned to me. I also studied Dhamma and memorised chants in order to participate in any religious ceremonies. Aside from one meal a day, I was allowed to smoke and to drink tea, chocolate and coffee.

It wasn't easy living the ascetic life but I'd like to think I did a good job. The greatest difficulties presented themselves when young women greeted me with morning offerings in nightwear that left little to the imagination. This proved especially difficult when they were kneeling before me.

The method outlined for the receiving of alms meant I could only stop to receive offerings if I was invited to do so by a layman; otherwise I had to continue walking. I couldn't be picky about the offerings either, which meant there were some interesting meals to be had. Whatever was given was mixed into a common pot: sweets, curries, noodles, and fermented fish created the day's meal. A layperson had to kneel before me in order to pay their respects as this stance reflected a lower and more humble status. He or she then joined their hands together in a prayer-like gesture before gently placing the offerings into my bowl. After they'd *wai*'d, I chanted a short blessing. I'm ashamed to confess that I frequently glanced at the women's cleavage during this process. Though afterwards, I suppressed my sexual desires by meditating on dead, rotting corpses while pondering the state of dirty human bodies, containing toxins and waste. I reminded myself that beauty fades and all human beings eventually wind up as decaying corpses. This method of suppressing sexual desire is known as *plong sangkhan*, and it helped me stay my course.

I somehow managed to survive three months at the temple without allowing a drop of alcohol to pass my lips. I think the fact I didn't have any drinking buddies definitely helped. I mulled over my life as I'd lived it up till then and justified my habits, thinking Lord Buddha didn't disapprove of social drinking in itself, but rather the consequences of drinking excessively. If you get so drunk that you lose consciousness, then who knows what could happen afterwards. I'd been involved in countless disasters over the last few years, and yet never seemed to get the point—even during my meditations.

However, by rigorously resisting the temptation to drink and other vices, the fog that had clouded my mind as a result of bad living gradually began to lift. I adhered to all 272 precepts laid down by the Buddha except one: after a long, hard day of labour, my stomach growled hungrily for sustenance, so I insisted that a temple boy boil water to prepare my instant noodles. I considered this breach of eating only one meal a day mild in comparison to some of the other monks' transgressions. For example, there were those who would speak directly to women, even going so far as to flirt with them.

Despite my noodle snacks, when it came to the sexual appetite, I was a lot more disciplined. I didn't touch or pleasure myself at all during my time at the temple. Hard labour helped to discharge my sexual energy, although I couldn't control my wet dreams. Afterwards I'd absolve myself of sin by reaccepting the Buddha's precepts and seeking forgiveness for my wrongdoings.

I didn't witness homosexual activities amongst the monks during my ordainment but, during my go-go-boy years, I heard all kinds of stories from my gay co-workers of how they had casual sex with other monks. Others claimed that their first male-on-male experience had transpired during their ordainment. It sounded highly plausible since they were all cooped up together and denied the company of females. As much as I could understand the need for sexual gratification, it was forbidden, and as a holy teaching I highly respected it.

During my first few weeks in the temple, I failed to comprehend the true significance of a beautiful lady who regularly paid respects to the abbot. I thought she was simply an extremely devoted Buddhist and enjoyed discussing the teachings with him, much like our elders; or perhaps she was just deeply troubled. I assumed the abbot acted as a spiritual guide for her just as any good monk ought to be.

As time went on I grew suspicious of the daily visits. Whenever she appeared on the scene the abbot would abruptly order us to get to work. The visits lasted several hours, and I didn't think it was possible to be that badly in need of spiritual guidance. Anyway, it's inappropriate for a monk to be alone with a woman, especially in his quarters. So the other monks and villagers soon gossiped about these strange prolonged visits. I learned she was a widow whose husband had died in an accident leaving her to rear their child. The suspicious tryst was exposed when she arrived at the temple one day clearly pregnant. Shortly afterwards the abbot unceremoniously left the monkhood to become a father and husband. While the rest of us monks had been working hard for the benefit of our souls, our leader was busy sinning. It was a disconcerting thought to say the least.

You can't take everything at face value. The people I was taught to hold in high regard—teachers, the police, and monks—were not always paragons of virtue and respect. Many simply used their positions to do whatever they pleased under the cloak of authority and, as long as they didn't get caught, they were happy to continue doing so. Even though I'm definitely no saint,

I'm at least somewhat honest about my weaknesses, which is more than can be said for these hypocrites.

During the last few weeks of my ordainment, I realised the religious path was not for me. At funerals and merit-making ceremonies, I began sneaking glances at young women from behind my talipot fan (a palm-leaf fan used by Buddhist monks while chanting prayers before a congregation). I was supposed to be concentrating on my religious duties but my mind was clearly elsewhere. Occasionally, these women would make eye contact, which caused me to quickly look away in shame. However, their coquettish image would be imprinted on my mind long after they exited my field of vision. I thus began to feel awkwardly embarrassed wearing my saffron robe, for I knew that my behaviour was not becoming of a monk. Had I remained in the monastery any longer I eventually would've violated the precept forbidding sex which would've brought an unspeakable amount of bad karma onto me. It wasn't as if I hadn't accumulated enough of it already.

I found the monastery too restrictive, and I didn't possess the kind of patience or discipline required to adhere to such a lifestyle. It was time to go home. Although I missed the layman's life, I had no intention of returning to my old drinking and gambling ways—I didn't see the need to. Having completed the targeted three months of ordainment, I resigned. As I departed from the temple and my fellow monks, I was proud of what I'd achieved; and yet I felt conflicted. I was still panged by a feeling of being incomplete. I still had no clear plan as to what I should do with my life—I was just as lost as when I began my spiritual quest.

My parents couldn't conceive a plan either. Directionless, I couldn't remain in Sisaket—so fate forced me to head to Bangkok. My sister had been working in the capital for several years and I invited myself to stay with her until I found a job and was able to get on my feet.

This was a starting point at least, and it seemed the most natural path to head down.

CHAPTER 7

The nurses are moving my bed. This is a good omen for only the most critical cases are situated next to the nursing station. I had the honour of being in first place for a long time. Now I'm being relegated to a corner next to the smelly bathroom, far from the nurse's sight.

The move makes sense; my condition has been improving slowly and now I can finally say that I'm on the road to recovery. However, I suspect that my loud and incessant complaining may have also played a part in my relocation.

I've good reason to complain though; some of these so-called caregivers seem disgusted by me and treat me with disrespect. I presume that they've easily guessed my profession. They don't seem to consider me a patient worthy of sympathy; only a ruffian who has simply collected his karmic come-uppance. But this time round I was not the instigator of the fight, well not entirely anyway. I was the one maliciously attacked.

I wonder if my life would've been better if I had remained in Sisaket. I could have given academia another chance; or tended to the farm and run the family business. Maybe I could've raised a family. If I'd had the strength to ignore the ridicule of the villagers and concentrated on reforming myself, things might have been different. If only . . . when joined together those two words have to be the saddest in any language; yet I find myself saying them on a daily basis.

When faced with criticism in the past, my usual reaction would be to run away. I preferred to embark on a journey into the unknown rather than face my troubles. So shortly after leaving the monastery and heading for Bangkok, I still didn't know how ill-equipped I was to survive in the city. I had no skills or qualifications that might have secured me a decent job, let alone the strength of character to resist the temptations that were everywhere on offer.

My sister Nitiya had been working at a Chinese restaurant in the City of Angels for many years. Her employer provided her with modest lodgings, which she shared with her fellow waiter-cum-boyfriend. Nit, as I affectionately called her, was initially reluctant to let me stay in her flat, especially considering my track record. She finally relented, but only out of deep love for our parents and dogged persistence on my part.

So with my secondary school certificate in hand, I set about job hunting. After days of battling Bangkok traffic, getting lost down myriad look-alike streets, and dealing with scores of unhelpful people, I finally managed to secure work in a department store in Ramkhamhaeng. 'Ram' is a busy, noisy, polluted district to the north of Bangkok. It is comprised of crowded streets, stalls, restaurants, countless hostels and pigeonhole-sized apartments, mosques, malls, and a sports stadium. My job, a rather inglorious one indeed, was as a bagger at a cashier stand. For a mere 3,000 baht a month, I spent hours stuffing expensive purchases into glossy shopping bags for well-off impulsive shoppers. Needless to say, after I'd paid my transportation costs, rent, food, and bought the odd piece of clothing, I hadn't two baht to rub together by the end of the month. I prayed to Buddha that I wouldn't fall sick or get a toothache because I'd have had no choice but to put up with the pain.

After months of barely scraping by, I felt utterly frustrated. Humiliated by city life, my old weaknesses for cigarettes, booze, and partying returned with a vengeance. I could always rely on such distractions to elevate my mood. So I began to splurge my earnings on these indulgences, and relished the feeling of release they afforded me.

Age-old cultural expectations dictated that I should be the one my younger siblings came to in times of need, yet here I was seeking handouts from my sister to make ends meet. My dependence on her added to the heavy load she was carrying and she frequently reminded me of this. Her constant nagging eroded my masculine ego and any trace of sibling affection between us soon disappeared.

As a true Pinit, Nitiya was certainly fond of alcohol and could easily hold her own in the company of any seasoned drinker. However, when drunk she often became extremely rude and violent.

On rare occasions, Nit and I shared what could loosely be described as a 'bonding' session. One such session took place at a late-night food stall over plates of appetisers, which we washed down with copious amounts of cheap whiskey. I was in a gloomy mood and was grumbling about my lot in Bangkok. The more I whined, the more agitated my sister became. Suddenly, her face reddened and she exploded, drawing shocked stares from other customers.

'Shut up! I'm sick of you, you loser. Do something instead of complaining! Why don't you sell your body if you're so desperate to make money, huh? There's just the place down the road, and I'm sure they'd take you on.'

I was stunned. I couldn't comprehend why Nit, my own sister, would suggest such a degrading career. I hurriedly gathered my belongings, left Nit to pay the bill, and sadly headed off towards our flat. As I trudged along, my heart felt heavy. I tried to get to the root of Nit's callousness, but found no satisfactory explanation. So I turned instead to examining the actual content of her abusive tirade. As the first morning rays began to slice triumphantly through the gaps between the skyscrapers, it dawned on me that it was actually possible for me to conquer this metropolis.

I'd briefly dabbled in the sex industry in Pattaya, selling my body to secure food, shelter, and pleasure. The life of a go-go dancer had appealed to me back then, especially after I'd been intimate with Chris. I found myself repeatedly drawn to this kind of career, and since I'd technically already prostituted myself, what was the big deal? Circumstances in Pattaya hadn't forced me to consider it a full-time career. But here I was broke and living in a permanent state of humiliation. This was enough to cause me to consider making a career of it this time round.

In order to avoid further conflict when my sister eventually stumbled in, I pretended to be asleep. As I did so, I silently debated the pros and cons of this possible career move. I tried to imagine the worst scenario—dying of AIDS. But I thought if I died, then so be it: *mai pen rai*. I hoped I would have accumulated enough money to leave a small fortune for my parents and siblings. The money would recompense them for the hurt I'd caused and, hopefully, they'd finally be able to forgive me. Perhaps, if the inheritance was large enough, I might even be hailed a hero. The more I thought about it, the more I cultivated this delusion of myself as noble and self-sacrificing. But given I was willing to sacrifice myself for the good of my family, surely I was a hero?

I could only sleep in fits over the next few hours and eventually rose around midday. I left the house and headed towards the bar my sister had suggested. As I turned the last corner, my courage began to flag.

'What if they reject me?' I thought, as I paced past the bar a few times. Feeling like a fool, I finally mustered up enough courage to go inside. My eyes took a moment to adjust to the dark, dingy atmosphere as an overpowering smell of stale smoke crept into my nostrils. Most men would likely have done a U-turn the second they'd entered such a place, but I found the surroundings similar to the girly bars I'd frequented so I wasn't too discomfited.

The premises, a blueprint for just about every other go-go bar throughout the country, had a raised stage on the ground floor for dancers, a bar to one side facing the stage, and several tiered rows of seats. The overall effect gave the impression of a poor imitation wooden coliseum. I tried to picture myself dancing naked in front of cheering, or perhaps jeering spectators. While attempting to fight my fear the venue's manager and male *Mama-san*, Anek, approached me. He began to assess me with the keen eye of someone who'd clearly been in the business for years.

'Well, what do you want?' he asked sharply.

'Whatever you see fit for me, sir,' I replied.

'We have openings for dancers only! Still interested?' he asked, no doubt expecting me to make a beeline for the door.

'I'm interested,' I replied, lowering my eyes respectfully.

I prayed he'd accept me as nothing would've been worse than returning home empty-handed to once again face my sister's contempt.

'You're a bit on the short side,' the *Mama-san* continued, 'but I can see some good muscle there. You can start tomorrow.'

The job interview lasted barely a minute and I couldn't believe the *Mama-san* hadn't demanded to see my 'goods' before employing me.

The rules were clearly explained and simple enough. I had to turn up at the bar before noon to start work shortly thereafter. When I started out, the majority of the bar's clients were *farangs* but over the course of more than a decade I've witnessed a large increase in the numbers of Asian gay men, and even female clients, turning to the sex industry to satisfy their needs.

I was 23 years old when I first danced as a go-go boy. I arrived at the bar the following day and made my way to the locker room. After undressing down to my underwear, I was ready to go to work.

We weren't expected to purchase underwear from the management like dancers today; instead, we were allowed to market ourselves as we saw fit. Thankfully, despite nursing a woeful hangover, I'd had the presence of mind to wear clean, presentable underwear. Clean underwear or not, my debut as a male prostitute was difficult. My co-workers were relatively friendly though, and the gaudy lighting and blaring music created a party atmosphere, but when I took to the stage I couldn't bring myself to make eye contact with the audience. Instead, I stared at the floor and awkwardly bumped my hips to the music.

The bar had rooms on the upper floors where bar boys could take clients for quickies. It's rare nowadays for bars to provide such services; instead, go-go boys conduct their business in the guests' hotels. Although we started dancing around midday we usually didn't see a customer until a few hours later. At 2pm or 3pm, after clients had replenished their energies with a hearty brunch, they once again thronged to the bars in search of a little afternoon delight.

During a short break after the first round of songs, I ran to the bathroom hiding angry tears. I'd cockily thought that I could conquer the stage and emerge victorious with a wallet full of cash and no qualms. I couldn't have been more wrong. No matter how much I tried to dress the job up and go out with guns blazing, it was degrading, and there was no denying it. I shoved my fist into my mouth to muffle my loud sobs. I bit down hard on my knuckles and welcomed the distraction the pain offered me. I wanted to be a person of value and significance, but instead I was reduced to a mere commodity. I had no excuses; opportunities in life hadn't been cruelly robbed from me by poverty, I'd simply thrown them away.

I couldn't bring myself to leave the bathroom. Every fibre of my being rebelled at the thought of dancing on that neon stage, and becoming part of that vulgar meat market.

My mind teemed with questions. What if my parents found out about my new profession? How badly would they take it? Would Pa finally reach breaking point and disown me? Was I freely handing the neighbours yet another opportunity to ridicule and shame us? I began to buckle under the weight of it all.

I was rudely brought back to reality by someone rapping loudly on the stall door, barking that it was time to get back on stage. So wiping my tears and suppressing my anguish, I strode back onto the stage.

Soon after my ignoble return to the spotlight, a client 'bought me out'. He was a nicely dressed, chubby American in his late forties. During one of the rare moments that I lifted my gaze from the floor I noticed his intense stare. He obviously knew bar protocol. He beckoned Anek and requested that I sit with him. My heart was in my mouth as I stepped down from the stage and made my way over to his table. I sat down shyly beside him as Anek began negotiating a deal. Even if I was blind, I could've sensed how turned on he was. His hands moved to my underwear, and he deftly slipped his fingers under the waistband and began rubbing my penis.

Meanwhile, Anek asked whether or not I was willing to oblige the client. I could have said no—I had a choice; I could have run out the door and never looked back, but instead I said yes.

I timidly headed upstairs with the American. He was beaming as his prize for the evening dutifully trailed behind him. I knew that with each step, I was moving further away from any vestige of innocence I had left. I was about to pass the point of no return, yet I kept on walking.

As soon as we entered the room, the *farang* grabbed a hold of my briefs and whipped them off, before pushing me onto the bed. He seemed to be doing everything at speed in case there was a danger I might run off. He started to 'smoke' me (a euphemism for giving fellatio). So far, the encounter mirrored those involving Loed and Chris. The American was not as easy on the eye as Chris, but his technique was surprisingly far better. He swallowed my manhood with voracious appetite. Then he began to kiss me teasingly whilst circumnavigating my body, all the while his fingers were paying special attention to my nipples. He teased every nerve, muscle and sinew, which caused me to cry sonorously as if I were a musical instrument. As my moans reached a crescendo, the American began a tune of his own until eventually we exploded together blissfully. Afterwards, he cradled me closely in his arms. Finally, I got up, showered and prepared to go back downstairs.

That was it; we were done. I was amazed that I'd enjoyed the experience as much as I had.

After paying the bar 500 baht for the room, he handed me 1,500 baht. I thanked him and took my leave. Looking at the three 500-baht notes, reality struck. This money was tax-free and it was half of what I earned in a whole month working at the department store. My terror from earlier evaporated as I wondered why I hadn't chosen to work as a go-go boy sooner. They say that money has wings; but in my case, the money gave me wings and allowed me to take flight, away from my many worries—at least for a time. A business cog began spinning in my mind—or maybe it was simply greed, but I found myself projecting how much money I could make in a year. I'd been searching high and low for an easy money maker and all the while it was right here in my underwear.

Things were certainly looking up. Not only had I gotten lucky with an easy client on my first tryout, but I was also impressed by the hospitality of my co-workers. I took an immediate liking to one in particular. Tae was an experienced go-go boy who carried himself with an air of confidence as if he were the most important person at the bar. His sanguine personality made him friendly and highly generous. I had asked him to spare a cigarette and instead of offering me one, he handed me a full pack of Marlboro. I was taken aback. He simply shrugged his shoulders and quipped that he'd plenty more. Tae bought me a beer to congratulate me. He told me that being bought out on one's first night was a good omen, a sign of bigger and better things to come. At the end of our shifts, we joined forces with several other boys and went out to continue the celebrations.

As we sat in a good restaurant studying the menu, I realised that I was no longer limited to the cheapest options. When it came time to settle the bill, Tae refused to let anyone pay for their meals or drinks. He then theatrically produced a thick wad of bank notes; we all stared on in stunned silence as he fanned them out to count the correct amount to give the waiter.

'Tonight is on me, brothers!' he boasted. We played along by calling him *luk pi*, or 'boss' and by buttering him up with feigned coos of admiration.

Once we were sufficiently drunk, my new friends began boasting of how much they made each night.

After exhausting themselves with self-flattery, the boys decided it was time to put me on the spot. They probed me by asking exactly what I would be willing to 'give up' to my clients.

'Would you be willing to allow a man's rod up your *pratulang*, that is, the 'backdoor'?'

Without hesitation I joked, 'I'm a jack of all trades and nothing is impossible for me!'

I was a fast learner and mastered the art of seduction with little effort. For Thais, body language and tone of voice are extremely important when interacting with others—the movement of an eyebrow alone can communicate a great deal more than words ever could. These cultural traits helped me improve my techniques. I'd learned much from the prostitutes I'd slept with and found that men were susceptible to pretty much the same style of seduction as women. On stage, I'd scan the room while lithely undulating my oiled body to the rhythm of the music, seeking out a target who hopefully had a large wallet. If he was clean and well dressed, I presumed him to be wealthy.

Once I'd chosen my mark, I'd look deeply into his or her eyes and begin suggestively licking my lips. If they showed interest, I'd stroke myself through my briefs with a carefully measured balance of coyness and confidence in order to give the impression that I knew how to give pleasure. I would follow this appetising exhibition by giving a playful, almost childish wink. If a client remained engaged, I'd give them a nod and fondle my crotch all the more. Sometimes, if I'd imbibed enough Dutch courage, I would teasingly reveal my penis and stroke it until it was fully erect. If all went well, this performance would capture the attention of a would-be lover. It would then only be a matter of time before the *Mama-san* paired us up. *Farangs* who selected me told me they did so because they found me boyishly cute. The irony was that prior to working in bars, my below-average height had always worked against me and was a source of profound insecurity. When teased about this, I usually became angry and violent and was determined to set out and prove I was a real man. In the bar world, a lot of men liked young, delicate boys. To Westerners I looked like a teenager. It didn't bother me in the slightest that they saw me as a child with whom they eagerly wanted to have sex. My role was to fulfil their fantasy—whatever that fantasy might be.

It didn't take long to adapt to my new profession. I knew it was illegal, but customers didn't come to bars under duress; they willingly paid for my services. My profession may not be entirely honest but it definitely shouldn't qualify as criminal. Thankfully, I've never been before a judge or been in prison because of it. Buyers and prostitutes negotiate their own terms based on mutual consent. Prostitution is against the law in Thailand, yet there are innumerable red-light districts. Entrepreneurs in the sex business tend to appear in the guise of everything from barbers to taxi drivers. One does not have to go far to find what one wants. Besides, if you walk down Silom Road, there are unlicensed vendors selling pirated CDs/DVDs, including porn, and brand-name counterfeits in broad daylight, 365 days a year, and they don't get arrested. We all do what we have to in order to survive.

Buddhism forbids promiscuity. It's sinful to sleep with countless partners, let alone clients; but I'd rather sin than go hungry and be forced to steal to fill my belly. The one thing that's bothered me most about my work is the amount of dishonesty involved. A great level of pretence was always necessary, especially when dealing with male clients.

CHAPTER 8

During my first week as a go-go dancer, I was bought out every day. I was a fresh face and everyone wanted a taste of the new kid on the block, or the stage as it were. I was a superstar, or at least I believed I was—a short-lived delusion harboured by most newcomers. I was receiving an average of 1,500 to 2,000 baht for each 'quickie'. Although considered unwise from a business point of view, I never actually specified a set price for my services.

'How much you pay is up to you,' I always told my clients.

Believe it or not, I sometimes got more than the going rate. My minimum fee was 1,500 baht, but if I struck gold, I could earn 4,000 baht and more. If a client happened to be stingy then I had no problem demanding a fair price.

With my wallet bulging, my self-esteem climbed and continued to do so, as if propped up by the interest and affection that the *farangs* were showering upon me. I felt for the first time in ages that my life was going somewhere.

I worked diligently at seducing men with my come-hither looks and sexy dance moves, which caused *farangs* to follow me upstairs two or three times a night. As a result I had no problem funding my expensive social life.

After a month of bar work, I still hadn't had anal sex. I'd made a point of being upfront with customers, telling them, 'I am not bottom boy. I don't put in mouth too!' As time went on I grew accustomed to the scene and relaxed somewhat. I started to have fun, and became more intimate and experimental with male clients. After a string of easy-to-please fellows, things turned a lot raunchier. I began to allow clients to insert their fingers into my anus, and occasionally, *farangs* would lick and suck my anus in order to stimulate me. I must admit that I found it strange but went along with it. The most mind-boggling foreplay I ever encountered was men sucking my toes. We Thais consider feet the lowest part of the body, almost unholy; they shouldn't be pointed at others or even played with, no matter how clean they appear to be. Sucking on them like lollipops—now that was just plain bizarre.

My clients sensed I'd become less inhibited and began asking me to do all sorts of crazy things, such as ejaculating into their mouths or all over their faces. Others requested that I urinate or even defecate on their bodies. I couldn't comprehend how anyone would find such base acts pleasurable. I could only shake my head confusedly while trying not to laugh in their faces. I began to put my personal feelings aside, and did whatever was asked of me, no matter how dirty or insane I thought it was. If the price was right then I wasn't going to run the risk of offending them with a refusal. Besides, the customer is always right, right?

Despite the multitude of perverse acts I participated in, I generally found *farang* men civil and reasonably respectful, unlike some of their Thai counterparts, who made no bones of openly criticising my services to their friends. *Farangs* didn't treat me as a lesser being just because I was a go-go boy; furthermore, I could freely express myself with them and so sought them out over Thais. When passing *farang* clients on the street, I'd wave, greeting them enthusiastically and they would always respond cheerily. I never felt the need to be shy or reserved around them, and they often hugged and kissed me as if we'd known each other all our lives.

They were also generous. If I told them I was low on cash they'd give me a few hundred baht, without expecting anything in return. In my eyes, the fact that they dressed well, behaved like gentlemen, and had bottomless wallets, made them seem like higher beings. I couldn't understand why they were attracted to me. Why didn't they want to be with beautiful women? Why me? Were they crazy being attracted to people of the same sex? They should have been rearing families and leading traditional lives.

I therefore came to see my body as an asset—something to be capitalised on, and did whatever I thought necessary to make it more attractive. I bought expensive clothing and accessories and only drank and smoked high-priced brands to further enhance my image. For a while I exercised regularly and ate health food to boost my stamina. Clients often wined and dined me at fancy restaurants and I happily soaked up the opulence. I would have had to save for months to afford one night in a five-star hotel in my former days; but now I stayed in them regularly.

My income was substantial at this point so I didn't see the need to curtail my spending. I also ignored my financial responsibility towards my parents; although, when my guilt grew too large to ignore, I'd send a token gift to them. I started to spend money faster than I received it. A night of partying would see every last satang spent. So, until I could secure another client, my meals would consist of cheap instant noodles.

I had learned to reciprocate my clients' 'affections' by giving handjobs and by kissing and nibbling their bodies, but I soon realised that if I wanted to remain in demand I'd have to be willing to do more. I reasoned that if the tables were turned, I wouldn't be very happy if I bought a girl who was selective about what she did or didn't do in bed. So I believed I had little choice but to perform fellatio and engage in anal sex. I'd previously feared that such acts would turn me gay; however, if compensated with enough beer and money, I could get through almost anything. I can't recall in detail the first time I performed oral sex on a man because I was drunk; however, strangely enough, I will never forget the meal I had after it. After business was finished, I went out with co-workers as usual; but my mood changed the second I began eating. Whatever I put in my mouth reminded me of the smelly piece of meat I put there earlier. I then remembered how revolting I found it, gasping for breath, while his organ pushed in and out of my mouth. When it was finally over, I ran to the bathroom and rinsed my mouth thoroughly, yet I couldn't get rid of either the aftertaste or the mental impression of what had transpired. Alcohol was the only thing I found that helped to erase part of the revulsion, so I ordered more beer. I never let anyone ejaculate in my mouth again. In future, when I sensed a client was about to climax, I'd use my hands to finish him off.

Most of my straight co-workers—and yes there were quite a few of them—detested receiving anal sex. Although they never admitted to it, I was sure they, nonetheless, occasionally overlooked this for the sake of receiving extra cash. I assumed they were like me in that respect. If you can believe it, despite having worked in this line of business for many years, I have rarely been the receiver of anal sex; more often than not in fact, I was the giver. How I managed to get away with this while still getting regular, long-term clients astonishes me.

My first attempt at being a 'bottom man' was neither pleasant nor consensual. I went back to a client's room after we'd spent the evening wining and dining. I ended up drunkenly crashing out face-down on his large bed. I was awoken from a deep sleep by a stabbing pain in my behind. The client had taken advantage of my inebriated state and had penetrated me. Despite the fact he used lubricant, it was still horrendously painful. The worst part of all was his violating me without a condom: for all I knew, he could have had AIDS. I struggled to free myself but he was on top, bearing down on me with his full weight, with one hand clasped around my neck to secure me. I thrashed about wildly causing him to penetrate me deeper while he pushed my head further into the pillow to stifle any resistance. I was gasping for air and groaning painfully as my legs and arms flailed about wildly. I began to curse intermittently between pleas for him to stop, but my resistance coupled with his obvious domination only heightened his pleasure as he panted harder and faster. I prayed he'd ejaculate quickly so the horror would end. My powerlessness obviously aroused him, and he thrust wildly as if to hurt me even more until finally unloading inside of me. After dismounting, he walked away as if I was a crumpled rag he'd just discarded. I was stunned. Yet I managed to quickly dress and escape without even a thought of being paid. When I returned to my apartment I scrubbed and headed to the safety of my bed. I lay there miserable; in pain and shock, hoping I hadn't caught a disease. I'd been raped, but as a bar boy I didn't feel I had a right to complain—it was part of the job.

Over the next few days I was scared to have a bowel movement in case I worsened the damage. I eventually went to a VD clinic to get my blood tested: fortunately, I tested negative.

Afterwards, and only once in a blue moon if I really liked a client, I had no qualms about sitting on his penis, but I always insisted he wear a condom. Occasionally, clients inserted dildos into my rectum, which although was not very pleasant, was still better than the real thing. I found being the giver of anal sex far less complicated; and once I got past the odour, I didn't mind playing an active role. If both parties are attracted to one another then sex with a male client becomes less of a chore, and can even be enjoyable.

After an endless catalogue of clients, and hours spent in gay bars, I began to develop a slightly effeminate persona. This manifested itself especially in the way that I walked and talked, which was a total U-turn as compared with the aggressive and masculine front I projected when living the life of a gangster and thug. I hadn't quite bought into the myth that bar boys could be turned gay once penetrated, yet I caught myself mimicking the behaviour of my effeminate co-workers. At first, I'd been consciously doing so for comic value, but when these mannerisms became natural, a habit even, I grew worried. I knew a few co-workers who, after receiving anal sex, had become *kathoeys* (transgender males), or turned gay, despite fiercely asserting their heterosexuality previously. They went from being husbands and fathers to being make-up wearing, female caricatures of their former selves. I was afraid that perhaps the myth was actually true after all. I tried to allay my fears by telling myself that I was flexible; able to play for both teams rather than just limiting myself to one.

A friend even took me aside and pointed out that he'd noticed the change in me and that he was also worried. He said if I didn't get a 'fix' soon then it was only a matter of time before I'd be playing for the opposite team. Taking his advice seriously, I set out for Patpong to find a compliant female prostitute, which was easy enough to do. I enjoyed the sex immensely, and my fears were therefore laid to rest.

I was relieved to discover I was not gay. I couldn't imagine visiting my home village as a homosexual, much less as a *kathoey*, when my reputation had always been that of a manly man. It would bring the greatest shame upon my family if I began prancing about openly; also, such an admission would lift the veil on how I was actually earning my living in Bangkok.

I continued to divide my affections between both genders so long as the players in question were attractive and paid me well. With men, I needed stimulation to get going but with women I could take the lead and attain an erection easily. Being with women was obviously my natural choice; somehow though, I find it difficult to explain my sexual orientation to men. Publicly, I'd never admit to anything but being straight; however, I generally do what feels good and right at the time. I suppose, to be honest, I am what Thais call *suea bai*, or 'bisexual'.

Once the confusion about my sexual orientation had been somewhat resolved, I made plans to pay a visit to my village, and to do so in great style. I bought the latest accessories and clothes especially for the occasion. When I stepped off the bus in Sisaket, I looked like a million baht. I was sporting a new designer hat, trendy sunglasses, a gold bracelet, an expensive watch, and boots that made the country folk drool with jealousy. My neighbours were obviously surprised at how much I'd changed. I regaled them with stories of the tens of thousands of baht I was raking in every month, working in an upscale hotel. It was a convincing alibi because I'd worked in hotels in Pattaya. The neighbours even complimented me on how sophisticated I looked, and the girls batted their eyelashes at me. No one could believe that the young, dirty delinquent they once knew had seemingly transformed into a handsome prince. I spent several months in Sisaket soaking up the attention and lavishing money on my fair-weather friends. Of course, the money eventually dried up, so I was forced to once again go back to work in Bangkok.

I returned to the city which by now seemed like home. Suddenly, I was feeling a lot more confident about my profession. I started taking the initiative, dealing with clients directly, and no longer using a middle man to negotiate for me. Well-rehearsed lines such as, 'Do you want to go with me?' or 'I like you, can I go with you?' dripped like honey from my tongue.

For the most part, life was good, if slightly routine. One downside though was the disapproving stares I attracted from other Thais when I was out with older *farang* patrons. 'Bangkokians' are generally good at hiding their contempt; but, in their eyes, I was the lowest of the low. I was a *puchai khai nam*—meaning 'he who sells his juice'. I forced myself to go against this cultural mindset by pretending not to care about what others thought. I comforted myself with the knowledge that I made far more money than most of them, and if they'd been aware of it, they probably wouldn't have been so quick to look down on me. At the end of the day, money speaks volumes. I have been in this business for years, and although most Thais still feel negatively about the sex industry, they've become more accepting as time has passed. I too have become more tolerant of people to whom I formerly wouldn't have given the time of day.

For example, with respect to gays and *kathoeys*, I now see them in a completely different light having come to understand them better. As a child, although I never bullied my effeminate schoolmates, I didn't see them as equals. Some of my *farang* patrons made me feel special because they respected me, and as a result, they taught me how to respect others. The industry changed me both inside and out, and it may be surprising to hear that I view most of these changes as being for the better.

In the past I would've liked nothing better than to provoke a fight, now I'd become content to clown around and entertain friends by making fun of myself. The need to act macho in order to scare away my rivals became unnecessary because I didn't consider them as rivals. Having come to view other men as friends and not competitors, I learned that it was possible and preferable for men to be civil to one another.

I thus became the life and soul of the party and people came to count on me for free beer and jokes. While I'd dispensed with my violent ways, some old traits remained, and I continued to gamble and drink heavily with friends after work. In other words, I still lived as if there was no tomorrow.

Although working in the gay scene had rescued me in a lot of ways, there were inherent dangers that, while I was aware of them, didn't prevent me from sometimes recklessly dancing my way in and out of bars, beds, and bosoms in Bangkok.

CHAPTER 9

My two younger brothers, Choke and Chamnan, on hearing of my 'success' from my parents, decided to come and visit me. They'd spent their energies slaving away in a factory for a measly 200 baht a day. They were fascinated by the fact that I'd secured such a well-paid job, and hoped I could advise them as to how to find similar employment. Our parents had invested so much money in my education that there was simply nothing left for my two younger brothers in Sisaket. Without an education, there were very few options available to them, and the prospect of working in a 'fancy hotel' for a good salary was therefore very appealing.

'I'm busy with my job. No spare time. I'm sorry, next time!' were some of the lame excuses I gave to postpone my meeting with them. In reality, I was ashamed and terrified they'd discover what I actually did for a living. When my parents had visited, I was only able to keep up the façade of being a hotel worker with the help of Nit. But Choke and Chamman forced a meeting when they simply showed up unannounced at the room I shared with my co-worker, Ton. As it turned out, it was my parents who had innocently given them the address. I felt that the game was up and I could no longer hide my terrible secret.

My appearance on seeing them, coupled with the sight of my co-worker, meant that on being confronted, I had no choice but to confess. They listened in stunned silence, looking disgusted and disappointed as the ugly truth unfolded. Finally Choke—the older of the two, and former member of my gang in Sisaket—spoke up.

'You have to be kidding,' he spat. 'I don't believe it. You, of all people, a macho delinquent, are letting men stick their *charuat* (rockets) inside you? It's impossible.'

I wasn't denying this, however, which spoke volumes. My brothers' respect seemed to dissolve before my eyes. My response was to become defensive, and I eventually responded by reproaching them for being naïve and judgemental. I jumped to my feet and began rummaging through my nightstand drawer. With a large wad of cash in hand, I began fanning my brothers with it, behaving like a proud lawyer who knew he'd just produced incontestable evidence that would surely win the case for him.

'Look how much I easily make,' I boasted. 'It's way better than working at your factory. Are you so stupid that you can't see the opportunities that are out there?'

I pontificated with the conviction of a prophet who had discovered the key to life's treasures.

'If you can bear men kissing and fondling you then you can make huge amounts of money. You fly your kite for free anyway, right? Why not let someone else fly it for you? And what's more, pay you for it?'

Just to hammer my point across, I dramatically whacked the fan of bank notes across their foreheads. As if magically enlightened, their disapproving expression transformed into looks of curiosity. The prospect of earning large amounts of 'easy' money captured their attention and began to intrigue them as it once did me. I enthusiastically boasted of the relative ease at which this money could be procured, then, in hushed tones, warned them that there were definitely unpleasant aspects to the job. Their smiles turned to frowns as the darker details came to light. But, just like a real professional, I finished my sales pitch on a high note.

'Essentially all you have to do is dance in your underwear, flirt with gay men and wait to be bought. The only part which requires any real talent is pretending you enjoy their company, and feigning pleasure if need be. You'll have to learn how to reciprocate affections in order to stay in demand though, and hopefully secure a long-term patron. The very least that would be expected of you is to give a helping hand to your client!'

I nonchalantly told my brothers that there was no risk of them getting pregnant, and therefore there would be no damage done to another human being. This, of course, was the same 'truth' my friends had used to persuade me to have sex with my teacher when I was a teenager. The moment these words escaped my lips, however, I suddenly realised that this logic had become a subconscious justification for all I'd been doing in the past years. A seed of misguided rationale had grown into a mighty tree that was now spreading its seed, giving rise to other young saplings.

My reasons for trying to persuade my brothers to become male prostitutes were two-fold. On the one hand, I genuinely felt sorry for them. I knew what it was like to try to make a life for oneself in the hustle and bustle of Bangkok. I also felt guilty for destroying their chances of success in life by robbing them of a decent education. I sincerely wanted Choke and Chamman to have a better life, but a career as a go-go boy was the only choice I had to offer. At least I didn't recruit them for commission as some of the bar girls do with their own friends and family.

Once they'd agreed to make a go of it, it wasn't hard to secure jobs for them—it was after all a seller's market at the time. The bars were constantly seeking new talent, and only ever requested copies of a boy's ID card and family registration papers at an interview. The *Mama-sans* would then give a candidate a quick once-over and decide on the spot whether to take him on or not.

Although Choke was 18, I'm not proud of the fact that Chamnan, my youngest sibling, had barely turned 16 when he joined my ranks. He was given a job at a bar that was notorious for its underage workers. After their stage debut, they recounted over rounds of beer how their legs were shaking like leaves as they tried to dance on stage; and how spasms of revulsion had run through their bodies as they slept with the men who had bought them, which was the most difficult part of all. Nonetheless, they were delighted at the money they made, which eased much of the nastiness they'd experienced. To my surprise, they even boasted how they'd commanded higher fees than I ever could on account of their youthfulness.

In the early days, my brothers often picked my brain on how to interact with customers. We quickly swapped afternoon shifts at the go-go bars in favour of night work. Adopting a similar work ethic, my brothers followed in my footsteps, soon gaining a reputation as being unreliable among bar owners.

Employers tended to use a reward system as an incentive to ensure their boys were not tardy. Dancers who turned up before 8pm received a 50-baht bonus while those who were late were fined an equal sum. Arriving late was a given for me, but I willingly forfeited the money. However, if a client bought me, I usually didn't receive that night's bonus anyway, so such petty rewards didn't really inspire punctuality. Conversely, the fine didn't bother me provided I met my target income for the night.

Even if a customer didn't buy me I could easily earn commission by cajoling clients into buying drinks. If a *farang* bought me a glass of Coke for example, the bar would charge him 200 baht and I would receive half of this. On rare occasions when I was both on time and relatively sober, I'd exercise to maintain marketability. The bar provided the necessary equipment that ensured its employees looked after their physiques. The workout was followed by a quick meal before the curtains were raised at 8.30pm.

My brothers had clearly been cut from the same cloth. We all worked a night or two at a time, then squandered our earnings in the same space of time, which forced us back into the bars to earn more cash. They never hinted at the emotional transition they must have gone through; after that first night they never even mentioned any of the pain, fears, or worries that went hand in hand with being a straight sex worker satisfying gay punters. On the surface at least, they seemed happy with their new jobs.

Unlike some of the female sex workers in Patpong, we weren't paid monthly. So we were free to move from bar to bar and this suited us down to the ground. We soon discovered that, as a team, our appeal was tripled, and before long we were making over one hundred thousand baht a month between us. This money poured through our hands like grains of sand, however, and it never occurred to us to try and repay any of our family's debts, or to build a new house for our parents like many others who worked in the industry dutifully did. We'd lived quite comfortably as children, but as adults the thought of sharing some of our new-found wealth simply didn't cross our minds.

The three of us were so similar in every respect that we were frequently mistaken for one another. Whenever one of us secured a client for the night, we'd ask him if he wanted the other two brothers as well. We could easily extract extra money from a client by creating a fantasy for him. On occasions when we were bought together we could make up to 10,000 baht in one go.

As the months passed, we managed to secure a long-term Australian sponsor named John who would become an integral part of our lives. I first met John at a go-go bar in Silom Soi 6. He was in his fifties, and seemed like a very friendly fellow. His friend Ron informed me that John was a former missionary—by that time nothing surprised me anymore. I quickly introduced John to my brothers who nicknamed him Santa or Papa John, on account of his kind nature. We enjoyed his company immensely and accompanied him on sightseeing tours such as Safari World, or to the ancient temples and ruins. We even brought him to visit our village.

During such trips, John would give me money to take care of the transportation costs and, in turn, I'd pack my pistol for protection in case thieves viewed the wealthy *farang* as an easy target. Of the three brothers, John was most fond of Choke, and he bought him a motor scooter as a token of his affections. His lavishness aroused the suspicion of our Sisaket neighbours, causing them to wonder just what role John played in our lives. When I think back on it, our poor parents must have had a lot to contend with after we returned to the city with John in tow.

After introducing my brothers to the love-for-money scene, I met a girl called Dao who was to become my first serious girlfriend. She worked as a traditional Thai dancer at an Isan-themed restaurant near Victory

Monument. My roommate Ton and I went together one night to unwind. Dao instantly caught my eye as she danced in a beautiful costume that seductively revealed her midriff. Her shiny black hair was pulled up in a small bun and secured with a long, thin hairpin. She was undeniably sexy, but traditional at the same time, which I found quite comforting. The restaurant sold tickets for five baht a dance, with the girl of your choice, for the duration of a song. To improve my chances, I boldly purchased ten tickets and tipped her handsomely after each dance. Meanwhile, Ton was busy courting Dao's friend Lawan, who was also a dancer, and over the next few days we invested much time and energy into winning their hearts.

One evening we invited them to sit with us. Neither of us had yet revealed our true professions and had pretended to be bellboys at upscale hotels. The two ladies began to open up to us: Dao told me that she was from Maha Sarakham, an inland province in the northeastern region of Thailand. She joked that when she first met me she thought I was a construction worker. She admitted that she'd been wary of me because of a scar on my right arm, which incidentally I got from a fight many years earlier. But money works wonders, and before long Dao began to overlook these apparent misconceptions. To prove my affections, I took out my wallet and flamboyantly counted out the princely sum of 1,000 baht, telling her it was a gift. She was overjoyed, and respectfully *wai*'d me by placing her hands and head on her chest, while profusely thanking me for my kindness. I was soon to discover, however, that Dao wasn't nearly as naïve as I'd first believed. That same night, Ton and I took our respective partners back to our room in Petchburi Soi 5 and made love to them. After we'd had sex, Dao began to act aloof towards me. It was obvious that she didn't like me as much as she'd led me to believe. The veil fell and I recognised Dao for what she really was—someone who was attracted to my money. I became suspicious that she might even be seeing other patrons, so long as the price was right. Rather than walk away from her though, I saw her as a challenge, and figured that if we stayed together long enough she might develop more genuine feelings for me.

So Ton and I asked our two lovers to move in with us. We didn't have a lot to offer: our quarters were cramped and all that separated our beds was a flimsy curtain. Sometimes, while both couples were having sex, I'd raise the curtain slightly and sneak a peek at the other pair of lovers, hoping to glean ideas for enhancing my own sex life.

The thought of Dao going out with patrons, particularly other Thais, drove me crazy. So I asked her to give up her job at the restaurant. I assured her that I was more than capable of supporting her. I believed money was the source of all happiness and thought that if I showered her with enough of it she'd know how much I cared for her.

When I reflect on what a large role sex was playing in mine and Ton's life at this stage, I am flabbergasted.

We went to work to have sex with our clients only to come home and have more sex with our girlfriends. Yet we never grew bored of doing it. In fact, I took pride in my ability to climax several times a day. For the most part, I viewed sex with clients as work; only on occasion would I derive pleasure from it—if they were attractive and I believed we were compatible for example, but with Dao I felt fulfilled on many deeper levels.

During the early stages of our courtship, I was quite insecure and became obsessed with winning her over. I would buy her beautiful clothes and gifts to keep her interested, but also so that she could continue being a showpiece that bolstered my public image. It was important that others see how well I provided for her. I gave her money on a daily basis to remind her how much I loved her, and even let her manage my finances, as most Thai husbands allow their wives to do. Unfortunately, Dao spent money as quickly as I did and we usually had next to nothing in our savings account.

Ton and I were very much in love with our girlfriends and went to great lengths to maintain our charade of being successful hotel workers. Inevitably though, the girls would eventually discover we were men of ill repute. One night, Ton's lover secretly followed us to our bar and, after discovering what we did there, had a huge blowout with him. Lawan rushed home to share the bad news with Dao. Thankfully, Dao responded more calmly. She quickly came to terms with this revelation and even assured me that she didn't mind because all that mattered was that I'd been so kind to her. While Ton and Lawan angrily broke up, Dao decided to stay with me. I was relieved, yet there was a part of me which couldn't help but wonder how she could possibly love a go-go boy. I came to the conclusion that it was because love is blind, and this was the reason she accepted me for what I was.

A few days later, it was my turn to be shocked as Dao announced she was pregnant. She'd initially been hesitant to break the news as she was unsure how I'd react. She timidly asked me if I wanted her to keep our child. I then began to understand clearly that it was desperation rather than love that bound her to me. I felt hurt that she only stayed with me for this reason, but on consideration, the amount of love I received from her was definitely disproportionate to the amount of money I'd invested. I had entertained the thought of Dao and I one day raising a family together, but that day had come far too soon. All I could see were the endless problems that came with raising a child. I was doing well financially, but our spendthrift ways ensured we couldn't afford to take on such a burden.

Realistically I wouldn't be able to give up my job for the child's sake either, especially when I was at the top of my game. In fact, I wasn't even sure if the child was mine. For all I knew, Dao could've been sneaking out to meet clients while I was at work.

What I dreaded the most though was the likelihood that I'd have to concede defeat and ask either Dao's or my own parents to rear the child for us. Raising a child in the countryside is naturally cheaper than in Bangkok, and many city-dwelling parents are forced to turn to their rural families for support when they're not making ends meet. If the neighbours discovered that I couldn't provide for my own child it would be a catastrophe. After selfishly considering all that I stood to lose, I became convinced that Dao had to get rid of her baby, and in the most matter-of-fact manner, told her as much.

Any glimmer of hope disappeared from her eyes, and she fell against the grubby apartment wall in floods of tears. She began howling miserably, so I squatted beside her and held her tightly to my chest. She was a million miles away though.

Exhausted, she stared vacantly ahead as I stroked her hair. Her energy levels suddenly changed though, and sorrow soon turned to anger as she struggled to break free of my embrace. She wildly began pounding her fists on my chest, demanding to know how I could be so evil. I grabbed her, terrified that if I let go, she'd leave me forever. I pleaded my case in an attempt to win her over to my way of thinking. 'It's been difficult to provide for two people, it'd be impossible to cope with a third hungry mouth. Think of it—we'd be poor and so would our child.'

I knew this reasoning would likely work—that the threat of poverty would terrify her. After a great deal of arguing, tears, and threats, she finally gave in. As the final threads of her resistance snapped, Dao breathed in slowly and deeply, as if to suck back in all the emotion she'd vented beforehand. I knew then that I'd never see those emotions again. She stood up, stared straight through me, and with steely determination, dressed herself, brushed her long beautiful hair and left our home without a word. She disappeared into the evening to search for the kind of medicine women take to induce a 'natural' abortion. I stood in the doorway, frozen but unemotional.

Abortion is illegal in Thailand, and backstreet 'clinics' are generally dangerous. There are ways around the law though. If a doctor agrees that giving birth could be life-threatening to the mother—and some doctors can be 'persuaded' to make such a diagnosis— then permission for an abortion would be granted. The other alternative is to buy large amounts of drugs that may or may not terminate the pregnancy. Dao went for the latter option.

She finally returned carrying a big bottle of *lao khao*, or 'rice wine', which she said was 'to help ease the guilt and speed up the abortion.' One hour later, she was squatting over the toilet as a stream of clots and blood poured from her. I fled the scene to stand on the busy street, nervously chain-smoking to keep any dark thoughts at bay. I knew with all my heart that it was better to not think too much about it; however, there was no escaping the fact that taking a life is a great sin in Buddhism. There was no going back though; this child was not meant to be.

When I returned, Dao looked frighteningly pale. She told me she'd successfully lost the baby; however,

I recognised that something else inside of her had also died. I couldn't heal the emotional scars she'd incurred, so I looked for ways to be of practical assistance. I soothed her with kind words while gently bathing her, assuring her all the while that everything was going to be okay.

I dried her off and brought her to our bed to rest, and while Dao fell into a fitful sleep, I snuck off into the night to buy my own *lao khao*. I did what I'd been doing for as long as I could remember—I steeped my problems in drink and refused to take responsibility.

It is only now, as I recall the event in my hospital ward, that I can see how truly wrong my decision was. Perhaps the tragedy that has befallen me in subsequent years, including the attack that has put me here, has resulted from my killing this unborn child.

It didn't take long for our relationship to sour. Dao resented me; she accused me of coercing her into taking the child's life. Whatever had transpired, she was no longer the person I'd fallen in love with in that Isan restaurant near Victory Monument.

Her bitterness was such that she would go out of her way to find any excuse to fight with and belittle me. We began avoiding each other, which was easy enough to do as the bar I worked in closed at 2am, so it was often close to dawn when I stumbled home. There were even nights when I didn't go home at all. I couldn't bear the feelings of guilt that were induced by Dao's accusations. I began to hate her for laying the burden of responsibility on my shoulders alone—why hadn't she taken precautions to prevent falling pregnant?

I felt defenceless. I was fleeing my troubles but had nowhere to escape to. When drunk, I tried to reclaim a sense of power by showing her who was boss. I became violent, and it needed only the drop of a hat to provoke me. It was I who paid the bills, so I insisted that she respect me. I became extremely jealous and didn't trust her. I was terrified she'd leave me, and I obsessed over the thought of her sleeping with other men behind my back. The more inadequate I felt, the more violent I became. For this was the only way I could think of to regain the control that was slipping away from me.

In time Dao's anger towards me transformed into fear. She was terrified of upsetting me and would tiptoe around to prevent triggering my next assault. During especially rough periods, she'd escape to her friend's house. I'd invariably come running after her, apologising profusely and promising to never hurt her again. I was always drunk when these bad 'incidents' occurred, and it was only when I sobered up that I would behave like the charmingly persuasive gentleman, after which she always returned to me. Unfortunately, my destructive alter ego always appeared when I drank, and so the vicious cycle continued.

There were many incidents that contributed to our eventual break-up. When we both began to suffer from excruciating pain whenever we urinated, a venereal disease was immediately suspected. VD clinics were easily accessible so we rushed off to one to find relief. It didn't come as much surprise when we tested positive for gonorrhoea. I suspected I'd either gotten it from one of my clients or from any of the bar girls I was seeing on the side. Dao reasoned that if I could give her gonorrhoea then it was only a matter of time before I infected her with a more serious disease. I begged her not to leave, promising that I'd be more careful in the future. Yet again she relented and stayed.

By this time stress and heavy drinking had taken its toll on me, which caused me to age incredibly. Things began to grind to a halt at work. Several slow days here and there turned into many slow months, until I was left with no choice but to ask Dao to return to work. She'd been a dancer before, and I felt that she could easily pick up her act and make us some money. I pitched the idea that she apply for hostess work at a Japanese bar in Soi Thaniya—a red-light district which catered to Japanese ex-pats and tourists. I wasn't as jealous of her sleeping with Japanese men. Thaniya girls were considered much more sophisticated than their Patpong counterparts, so at least I could boast I was going out with a Thaniya girl. Dao was highly insulted, however, that I'd dare suggest such a thing. She hadn't minded working to support herself in the past but she wasn't about to allow herself be pimped out by her sweetheart. She once more sought refuge at her friend's and I didn't see her for days.

One night 'Lady Luck' smiled on me and I earned 10,000 baht from a naïve client who'd obviously just stepped off the plane. I took my 'winnings' to a jeweller's and purchased a beautiful gold necklace as an act of contrition for all the pain I'd caused Dao. I knew exactly how to win her over, and she accepted the necklace with a bright smile and moved back in with me. The following day a few friends called by for a game of cards. I still had a few thousand baht from the previous night and I planned to clean them out. Dao usually regarded such visits as an excuse to get out of the apartment for a while. She claimed she didn't want to get in the way of our male bonding. I think it was more likely she couldn't handle our foolish behaviour. Either way it didn't matter; I was happy to spend time with the boys. We drank and played cards until all the money and booze was depleted. Broke and extremely drunk, I decided to take the necklace to the nearest pawnshop and exchange it for cash, believing I'd make a profitable comeback. Unsurprisingly, after more beer and several rounds of *pokdeng*, I lost everything. When Dao discovered I'd gambled her necklace away she was furious, and our relationship moved another step closer to dissolving.

The last night I saw her, I returned home drunk and in high spirits. Upon entering our room, I noticed Dao sitting on the floor; her knees were drawn up to her chest as she rocked back and forth with tears streaming down her face. She'd secretly returned to her old workplace where an ugly and elderly patron had convinced her to eat with him in a hotel room. When he had her alone, he had apparently raped her. I was livid, but I felt no sympathy for her whatsoever. I'd wanted her to work as a Japanese-style hostess and she refused, calling me a pimp, yet she'd secretly gone back to work at the dance hall. I doubted this was the first time she'd done so, and I wondered how many patrons she'd actually slept with. A torrent of rage issued forth and I began yelling at her: 'I forbade you to work at the dancehall. I don't want you sleeping with Thais. I don't ask much, and in return you disobey the one thing I wanted from you! I'm sick of you, you selfish bitch!'

With my pride wounded and my masculinity undermined, I fought, determined to make her hurt. I punched, kicked, and strangled as my arms and legs took on a life of their own. The neighbours must have heard us, but they didn't call the police. Fortunately Dao's screams, chokes, and desperate gasps for air did get someone's attention: mine. These sounds jolted me back to reality just in time. I'd nearly killed her. The second I released my hold on her throat she fled to the safety of a friend's house in a nearby *soi*.

I was inconsolable.

Was I just another client to her? Had she stopped loving me when I was unable to provide for her?

My whole life I'd been emotionally dependent on others—from my parents, to friends, and now my girlfriend. When Dao slammed the door that evening, I had a sinking feeling it'd be for the last time. I was right; we never spoke again.

A month later I heard she'd found a new lover who was older apparently, but rich. Our relationship lasted two rocky years, which should have been ample time to recognise the bad attitude I had towards women. I believed I loved them, but I wasn't capable of giving them the respect they deserved. I either loved or hated them according to what they did or didn't do for me. It was all about me.

If I were to meet Dao today I'd apologise profusely. She wouldn't forgive me though; of this I am sure. I believed my behaviour was justified; I was her provider and this entitled me to punish her for any acts of defiance, even with a punch or two. It's clear now that what I felt for her wasn't love, but instead a sense of ownership.

CHAPTER 10

After Dao left, I continued working in bars, but only sporadically at best. So I was forced to improvise. I found employment as a go-go dancer at a bar that was known for its highly explicit sex shows. The manager called me into his office one day and asked if I would be interested in performing for extra money. I readily agreed. He said that my *khong* was a nice size and shape, and since I wasn't shy I'd make a great showman. There weren't many performers back then because it took nerve to get up on stage and do the outrageous things we did.

I danced completely naked and with a fully erect penis, jerking myself rhythmically to the music. To maintain an erection, I used either a cock ring or a condom which I wrapped tightly around the base of my penis. This was often extremely painful but, as the saying goes, the show must go on. Ton and I worked together and we always performed in *phra*, or 'male', roles matched with *nang*, or 'effeminate male partners', in simulated anal sex. Once our act was finished, we roved about the audience collecting tips.

Occasionally the manager organised masturbation contests which were judged by how far or quickly contestants could shoot their semen. Before taking to the stage, the contenders were fed a hefty diet of porn to get them in the mood. When ready, the boys scrambled to their seats on stage and went for it wildly before an awe-struck audience. This kind of competition increased in popularity until it became a daily event that was used to draw crowds into bars.

At one such contest I met a ladyboy, or *kathoey*. This *kathoey*'s name was Lin and she became a long-term client. She was highly feminine with long, natural hair, fair complexion and a petite body. Her exceptional beauty won her many ladyboy beauty contests. She'd tease me by saying if I ever wanted to come and live with her, all I had to do was pick up the phone and she'd welcome me in a heartbeat. The income from shows was insufficient to live on, so, on a whim, I decided to take her up on that offer one day.

I temporarily quit the bar life and headed to Phanatnikhom in Chonburi Province to move in with her. Lin still had a penis as she hadn't undergone genital reassignment surgery, but she did have breast implants and a wonderfully curvaceous body. Things were great for us as I had no trouble assuming the male role in bed with her. It didn't matter that she still had a male piece because in every other way she was truly feminine. I never bothered to ask why she hadn't undergone surgery down there; she seemed happy with the way she was, and that was good enough for me.

I worked as a waiter, and helped Lin with the household chores while she managed a beauty salon in a well-respected hotel. Lin was reasonably well-off and she never denied me anything. Being of Chinese descent, and from a very traditional family, Lin first introduced me to her pa and mae during a formal dinner. If her parents disapproved of our relationship, or of Lin's identity, they certainly didn't show it. They were proud of Lin, as she had a good income and reputation. Due to her frequent participation in local charity events, she'd become a well-known figure in the community. I remember that she regularly cleaned the cemetery as a mark of respect to the dead. I suspected that Lin tried to compensate for any criticisms she'd received over her nonconformity by working extra hard to succeed and ultimately gain respect.

She proudly introduced me to her ladyboy friends at parties and dance clubs. I was certain that when it came to our relationship her motives were entirely pure; she really loved me and wanted to be life partners.

We lived together in Phanatnikhom for a month before moving to Pattaya where Lin opened a restaurant. I'd like to say that we lived happily ever after, but unfortunately that was not the case. I became bored with domesticity, and once again fell into the clutches of alcohol and bad behaviour. I started going out nightly with friends no matter how much Lin begged me to stay in with her. My heart was not fully invested in our relationship, and carousing with buddies appealed more to me than spending time with my girlfriend. So we eventually broke up.

Being conceited, I thought I'd be fine in Pattaya without her. I soon found, however, that work was hard to come by and thus defaulted to the one career for which there were always vacancies. It didn't take long to find work in Soi Pattayaland, which was known as 'boys' town' in the seaside resort.

The fee for sex at the time was approximately 500-1,000 baht, which was considerably less than in Bangkok. Saying this, the cost of living was also less, so I managed to make ends meet.

The manager of one bar I worked in offered me free accommodation at his premises for being a go-go boy/ sex show performer. As in Bangkok, each show lasted the length of a song or two, and I earned roughly 400 baht in tips.

My roommate, a ladyboy, was a former cashier who'd also worked at the bar. She'd slept with customers on rare occasions and sadly contracted HIV. By the time I moved, she had developed AIDS and was dying. In bars, you can be a doorman, barman or DJ, but you also have the option of selling yourself. Many of the staff had been go-go boys, even when past their prime, and they had no objection to selling their bodies when the opportunity arose. Those who joined as purely regular staff, more than likely ended up either dancing or turning tricks.

My poor roommate spent her days groaning uncomfortably on a mat while struggling to maintain her weak grip on life. It wasn't long before she would surrender to her condition. I saw the will to live seep out of her with each laboured breath. Her skin became dark and dry; she smelled terribly and was plagued by bouts of diarrhoea that turned her into little more than a skeleton. Her condition deteriorated daily and there was little I could do to help her, even if I'd wanted to. I slept in my corner, as far away from her as possible, terrified I might contract the disease. Her family finally came to collect her and I heard she died a week later. I found this experience traumatic; watching someone slowly and painfully fade away made me aware of my own mortality. AIDS isn't exclusive to any one sector of society, but working in the sex industry certainly placed me in a high-risk category.

I'd been in Pattaya a few months when the tourist season hit its annual low. Clients became scarce and money scarcer, leaving me with little choice but to head back to Bangkok where work was easier to find. I moved in with my sister Nit for a while as I couldn't afford a place of my own.

One day, shortly after my return to Bangkok, I went to Lumpini Park to jog and lift weights. As I walked to cool down after my workout, I noticed a woman reading a book under the shade of a large tree. I approached her and politely asked if I could have a sip of her water. She smiled and shyly nodded. She blushed as her hand brushed against mine while handing me the bottle. I asked if I could sit with her: she knew that I was coming on to her and seemed a little uncomfortable at first, but she soon became more relaxed. I found her surprisingly easy to talk to. While my interest in my ex-girlfriend Dao was chiefly driven by lust, with this girl, I found my heart seemed to flutter while talking to her. She introduced herself as Nuan, and although she was a tad plain for my liking, she was very kind and friendly. Dao had delivered a crippling blow to my male ego, but Nuan represented the hope that this self-confidence could be restored. I fantasised that we were two loners made for each other, and were destined to be together. Our meeting wasn't the work of pure chance: it was fate.

I lit a cigarette and, to my surprise, Nuan asked if she could have one too. As I lit it for her, our hands touched a second time, and Nuan did not pull away. Feeling emboldened, I took her hands firmly in mine and began making my intentions clear. I could tell she was flattered by my advances. We were overstepping cultural boundaries by being so openly affectionate on our first meeting. As a go-go boy, I was naturally a fast mover, yet it seemed it was Nuan who was eliciting these responses in me, not my desire to earn a few thousand baht.

She had the most melancholy eyes I'd ever seen. They had a magnetic pull from which my eyes found it impossible to look away. We quickly opened up to one another and exchanged thoughts, touches, and phone numbers. I imagined she was a damsel in distress, and I was the hero who'd save the day. Although I revealed a good deal of personal information, I lied about my

profession by saying I worked as the doorman of a
dance club in Silom Soi 2—a well-known gay area.

I asked Nuan to come back to my room, feeling
confident that she'd sleep with me. I thought that this
would strengthen our tie to one another for I sensed
she was the real deal.

After we'd had sex, the thought of Nuan leaving filled
me with dread. I couldn't bear being alone anymore. So
I asked her to stay permanently and she readily agreed.
At the time, Nit was visiting her boyfriend's family as
they were soon to be wed. When they returned home
later that evening I introduced them to Nuan, casually
mentioning that she'd moved in with us. Nit rebuked
me for letting my horniness be the reason for bringing
a stranger into her home. Her anger may have been
justified, but Nit went too far when she called Nuan
a whore. I knew she'd lost all respect for me long ago,
but to call my new lover such names was outrageous.
I barked at Nit to keep her foul mouth shut and
curtly told her we were on our way. In record time, I
packed my belongings and stormed out of the house.
We headed for the room Nuan shared with her friend
and there, likewise, she gathered her possessions. With
bags in hand, we set off to find accommodation. By
late evening we'd rented a 100-baht-a-day room in a
guesthouse. I confidently told Nuan to give up work
because, as her man, I intended to provide her a good
life.

I was 31 years of age when Nuan and I became a
couple, which—by go-go boy terms—is pretty much

over the hill. Customers bought me less frequently than they had in my heyday. I not only attributed this to age though, for I was convinced Dao had cursed me for forcing her to abort the baby and had therefore cast some sort of vengeful spell on me. I became terrified that the bad karma caused by the abortion was going to cause my being reincarnated as a lesser life form. Perhaps I'd come back as a mosquito, forced to spend its days avoiding being swatted; or a pig awaiting slaughter; or—worst of all—a foetus that was bound for abortion.

So when Nuan told me she was pregnant, I insisted she keep the baby, and never even discussed the option of terminating it. I'd grown very fond of Nuan and had no desire to lose her. She'd once worked in the catering section of a hotel, and the manner in which she kept our room clean as well as her ability to prepare delicious meals for me each evening more than substantiated this claim. I knew then she'd make a good partner and parent.

It was only a matter of time before Nuan also discovered what I really did for a living. She asked to accompany me to work one evening and, since I could no longer hide my secret, I agreed. She was shocked to discover I was a go-go boy.

'I don't understand why you lied to me!' she fiercely snapped.

'Don't make a scene. Had I told you the truth, would you honestly have stayed with me, huh?'

A long and uncomfortable silence followed. Both of us were waiting for the other to break it—to either make things right or close the door on our relationship forever. Nuan would be the one to break it.

'I'd have walked away without a second thought . . .' She touched her growing belly and sighed, '. . . but it is too late now. This baby needs a father and I want to do right for my child.

'Promise me that you'll find alternative work before its birth and to always be careful with clients.'

I solemnly swore and touched her stomach as if to pass the vow on to our unborn child. She wanted to protect the baby from disease as much as she could. I knew Nuan genuinely loved me because, child or no child, she was the type of woman who wouldn't stay if the reasons weren't right. From that evening on Nuan would meet me on the nights I wasn't bought by a client, and we would walk home together hand in hand until she was too heavily pregnant.

Nuan could handle me sleeping with male clients; however, she became jealous when I was bought by females. But in time she also came to terms with this aspect of my work. Her acceptance boded well for my professional life, and customers once again began buying me on a regular basis. It was as though the life force growing in Nuan's belly was somehow overriding Dao's curse.

While Nuan was heavily pregnant, Papa John asked me to stay with him at a hotel on Surawong Road for a few weeks. He thought I was gay and had no idea I had a pregnant partner. I was travelling back and forth between his hotel and my room. I couldn't stand living with John round the clock and would find excuses to spend time with my sweetheart. One evening I returned to Nuan in an especially jubilant mood as my pockets were bulging with the money John had given me. Watching TV together, Nuan mentioned she was feeling pain in her lower back. Her due date was still ten days off so we were hesitant about rushing off to Chula Hospital. However by 4am, Nuan's contractions began in earnest, convincing me that she was in labour. I ran downstairs to hail a taxi while Nuan dressed and packed her bag. Taxi drivers were refusing us because they were scared Nuan would give birth in their cabs. It was too early in the morning to get a bus, so we had no choice but to walk to the hospital. Eventually, a kind taxi driver saw us struggling along and kindly took us to our destination.

I was tired, excited, fearful, and overwhelmed all at the same time. With the money John had given me, I booked a VIP room for Nuan. The nurses very nearly sent us away saying that first-time babies are often overdue. But we refused to budge and so they had to give in. Our stubbornness paid off, as after a long labour Nuan gave birth to our son the following morning. I wasn't present at the birth though; Thai men generally prefer not to witness such events. Instead, I anxiously paced back and forth outside the labour room. And then the news came—I was a father. I didn't know how to react. Suddenly an incredible responsibility had been bestowed upon me.

Here we were at last, face to face with our precious little boy whom we named Chuan. I felt sorry for the poor thing. We weren't ready for his arrival and so had no clothes, bottles or any other baby gear. It's a bad omen to buy such things before the birth, so being superstitious we were unprepared.

Chuan was an adorable baby, and very handsome. But I was careful to ward off evil spirits by loudly proclaiming that he looked 'hideous and ugly'. By doing this I tried to fool the evil spirits so they would leave him alone. After the hullabaloo of the birth, I rushed off to Prathunam to buy baby clothes. Despite being over-excited, sleepy, and clueless, I managed to get five matching sets, albeit with the help of a shop assistant. I figured that would be plenty for the time being. When Nuan saw the clothes she laughed so hard the nurses warned her she might rupture her stitches. Apparently, the clothes I'd bought were more likely to fit a three-year-old than a three-day-old. She joked that I was trying to bury our son in an avalanche of oversized clothes. We ended up chuckling away and I confessed I was a little inexperienced to say the least. Nuan advised me to stick with moneymaking and to leave the baby rearing to her.

Papa John eventually discovered my family secret. He confronted me as to why I was always running off on him, and I had no choice but admit that I had a partner and newborn son. He took the news surprisingly well.

I was certain he'd feel angry or cheated but instead he asked to meet Nuan and Chuan and from then on he became a member of our small family. He was genuinely happy for us, he bought toys and gifts, and Nuan would often wrap Chuan up and take him to visit Uncle John at his hotel. He continued to support us and made our lives a great deal easier.

Buddhists believe the process of dying begins with the very first breath we take. I also believe that every birth is counterbalanced by a death, and vice versa. This proved to be the case with my family.

Shortly after Chuan was born, my brother Chamnan called to tell me that on their recent trip home, Choke was killed in an accident. Apparently, they had been drinking and joyriding with two mutual friends. Choke was squatting on the flat floorboard of the scooter John bought him while his two friends were sitting on the seat; Chamnan followed behind on his bike. They were racing like daredevils and none of them were wearing helmets or protective gear. It was crazy behaviour, but they were on quiet country roads and just assumed they'd be safe.

At that precise moment a teacher from our village was showing his wife how to drive his pick-up truck, but the woman lost control of the truck and went careening straight into Choke's scooter. Choke's body was tossed into the air like a rag doll and came crashing down onto the vehicle's bonnet. He hit it with such force his stomach burst open. He died upon impact. Chamnan, who witnessed the entire incident, was so traumatised he began vomiting uncontrollably. To this day, he is unable to erase the images of Choke's death, who was only 26 years old, from his mind.

Devastated by the loss, I diverted my energies into caring for my son. My parents and other siblings must have followed my example and flocked to see our new baby. I was brave for my son's sake, yet it was difficult to find distraction from the guilt I felt over Choke's death. After all, it was I who first introduced him to John, and it was John who bought Choke the scooter. If John hadn't become my brother's patron then he would've never met such an end. It was irrational to blame myself I know, but grief distorts logic. Karma works in mysterious ways. Why had this tragedy befallen Choke and not me? I can only think that I must have earned some excellent merit in past incarnations, and only these had kept me alive. John was so distraught over the loss of Choke—his favourite boy—that he distanced himself from the rest of us.

After Choke's death, Chamnan came to me for a chat. He hesitatingly said, 'I want to change careers, Chai. I'm done with selling my body; I'm sick and tired of the vicious cycle of being broke, earning, and then blowing it all, only to find myself broke yet again. I believe the money we earn from trading our bodies is cursed; it seems to have no value and if we're honest, we'll never be prosperous this way!'

I was incredulous. How could he leave his work and —most importantly—desert me? Especially after we'd lost our brother?

He patiently continued. 'I miss country life, brother. I want to invest the sweat of my body in something productive, something that will make me value what I earn and make me proud of my achievements! I've a job opening in Prachinburi at a shrimp farm. They provide accommodation, food, and yes, the salary is small, but it's regular.'

When I found out how much he'd earn, I exploded in a fit of rage. 'You're a fool to go to the backwoods of some nowhere province for only 5,000 baht a month even if the job's perks include a bit of food and a roof over your head!'

His final words broke my heart, for I knew they conveyed that he no longer respected me. 'Chai, I can't follow in your footsteps any longer. You've lost your way and I can't lose mine; I can't let you take what little opportunities I've left from me. If you were smart you'd join me!'

So with that, he left the sex-for-sale scene and I'd lost the love of two brothers.

I was devastated, but tried to remind myself of those who remained with me and the responsibility I had towards them. I had a loyal and understanding partner, and a young son who set my life ablaze with joy. I felt better for the fact that there were two people who desperately wanted me in their lives; and this always helped when the sadness of missing my brothers threatened to overshadow me. My financial situation was reasonable and I handed most of my earnings to Nuan, just as I had Dao; the difference being, Nuan was thrifty and so we didn't live beyond our means.

CHAPTER 11

I was unable to keep my promise to stop working as a prostitute on becoming a father and I kept dancing and hustling for several years afterwards.

It became increasingly difficult though to find clients in Silom Soi 2 so I opted for a change of scenery. I therefore moved to a very popular gay bar in Soi Twilight. Although I would never hear from Papa John again, it didn't take me long to find a new patron. He was an American called Thomas. We hit it off amazingly well and he soon asked me to be his boy. He shared a house with several *farang* friends to save on rent. I moved in as both the resident houseboy and a tourist guide and showed them around the usual sight-seeing destinations. The house was spacious and nicely decorated, but Thomas was not as generous as I'd hoped. He tried to keep me on a leash with an allowance of only 10,000 baht a month, which simply wasn't enough to raise a family on. Of course, I didn't tell him I had a young family and he most likely thought this amount of money was more than adequate for one person.

Leading a double life and travelling back and forth between Thomas and Nuan took its toll and I became increasingly stressed. I was trying my best to make more money especially considering how precarious my 'houseboy' position was.

Thomas didn't like me working as a go-go dancer and was eager to make our relationship exclusive. So I was forced to sneak out of the house either to go to work or to visit my family while Thomas was at work. I managed to visit Nuan and my son at least twice a week to give them what money I could.

We decided to let Chuan's hair grow and by the time he started preschool, he looked like Mowgli from *The Jungle Book*. His dark locks were always immaculately clean and he was always well-groomed for Nuan was an excellent mother. He attracted admiring stares wherever we went, and a wealthy Chinese silk-shop owner even went so far as to ask us to give Chuan to him. The *tao kae*, or 'rich Chinese businessman' and his wife desperately wanted a boy to carry on their family name. Although he had three grown daughters, all of whom were successful doctors, it was not enough for them. I reckon the *tao kae* was also attracted to my boy because I'm half-Chinese. For the Chinese, sons are treated with reverence, and Nuan and I knew that, had we given Chuan up, he would have led a very comfortable life. The *tao kae* even asked us to allow a doctor of physiognomy to examine Chuan. The theory behind physiognomy is based upon the idea that a person's physical appearance, particularly their face, can give a *sin sae* insight into his or her character and personality. Nuan and I didn't mind the *sin sae* examining our baby because we were more than a little curious as to what he'd say. Every inch of Chuan was examined, even down to the shape and length of his fingers. Eventually, the *sin sae* announced that Chuan would be an auspicious addition to the *tao kae's* family.

At first, Nuan and I were flattered that such a respectable family wanted to adopt our child but their pleas were incessant and eventually became annoying. Nuan finally refused to listen to them anymore. She informed them politely that Chuan was her son and that she would raise him, however difficult it may be.

Although this type of adoption is not common practice in Patpong, it does happen. Bar girls, for example, would sometimes offer their children to business owners or other prospective buyers but were mostly turned down. Considering the number of unplanned pregnancies, there are plenty of children on offer. But certain 'good people' generally fear that a child born to a prostitute or to any bad blood might bring misfortune to their household. I completely understood why many women wanted to give up their children. Not only were they not prepared for the additional responsibility, but I don't think they relished the thought of telling their child how they had come into being. To top it off, they weren't in a position to give up prostitution, for most have no other option. I'd been in a similar position when I asked Dao to abort our child. Things hadn't improved that much more when Nuan fell pregnant, but our feelings for one another were strong and this strength was the glue to hold our little family together. The first time I laid eyes on my precious baby I made a promise that I wouldn't fail him or his mother. I'd already failed so many people, but I was determined never to fail my family.

One night at the go-go bar, I met a Dutchman named Erik. He sat with a Thai woman who I assumed was either his girlfriend or a guide helping him to procure a man. On what I considered lucky occasions, I was bought by couples and ordered to pleasure the wife while the husband lustfully looked on. In this case, I assumed that Erik was gay so I directed my attention towards him. He became increasingly uncomfortable, though, and finally explained that he wasn't actually gay but did need a man to star in some porn movies. It seemed that I was the man he was looking for. The Thai woman, who turned out to be his wife, introduced herself as Wan and complimented me on my clean-looking and nicely shaped *khong*. Erik was promising 35,000 baht a month for my time, so I wasn't going to turn down an appointment to meet at his hotel on Sukhumvit Road to discuss the job in more detail. I was surprised by my good luck and congratulated myself for having stumbled upon this golden opportunity. My earnings from the bar, even when combined with Thomas's allowance, weren't enough to cover the expenses of two adults and a child, not to mention the little extra I wanted for myself.

The following day, I met Erik in the hotel lobby. We bought a few beers and took a seat in a secluded corner. He assured me that his porn films would only be distributed on the Internet via a subscription website based in Holland. From the start he was upfront about what type of pornography he wanted to produce. He told me that the best adjective to describe it was 'unconventional'. He wanted to film Thai women 'playing' with human excrement, urine and vomit; and also have a dog feature at some point in the movie. My face instantly registered utter disgust. Erik then quickly affirmed that the camera would be focused on the women the majority of the time, so I needn't worry too much. Most of the subscribers would be logging on to view the women anyway, not the men. My gut instinct was to just get up and walk away, but Erik pleaded with me to think about it, saying that he needed someone with my talents. I excused myself to go to the bathroom.

I went over the proposal in my mind several times. Finally I concluded that since I'd participated in so many other less-than-desirable activities through the years, what difference would one more make? It wasn't as if I was some sort of fairytale character—I think Buddha must have been all out of happy-ever-afters by the time I reached the top of the queue. I began to recall some of the scenarios I'd gotten myself into over the years.

Once an African client asked if he could penetrate me but I saw that his manhood was far too big. So he asked me to give him oral sex instead, but I couldn't fit his penis into my mouth without half-choking on it. So in lieu of fellatio, I used both of my hands to literally wrestle with his monstrous piece which I licked from base to tip to help speed up his climax. He was a gentleman though and respected my limitations, but the taste and odour made my stomach turn. In my experience, not all black men are well endowed, but this man was definitely well above average.

I also remember a very strange, clean-cut *farang* who used to hang out in the bar's toilet. He'd approach go-go boys and offer to pay them to urinate into his mouth while he masturbated. I'm not kidding—he actually paid to drink our urine. We go-go boys used to roar with laughter whenever we talked about him and used to look forward to our toilet sessions. He became so well-known, in fact, the second he turned up we'd all start ordering large beers. While he preferred younger boys, he was willing to give 200 baht to anyone streaming their pee down his throat. Some boys managed to make three or four rounds a night and so made up to 800 baht. Hell, some of us saw these trips to the bathroom as a way of paying for our beers. The small toilet area would often be crowded with snickering bar boys lining up to empty their bladders for a fee. I've seen him around different bars over the years and he still appears healthy despite his strange fetish. It was bizarre indeed to see his eyes light up as soon as my bladder started to empty. He later wised up though, and lowered his price to a much more modest 20 baht a shot.

I also remembered that clients would sometimes ask me to get them *ya ba*, or amphetamine pills, which were relatively easy to find in the days before Prime Minister Thaksin's war on narcotics. Once upon a time, it was just a few baht per tablet and they could be purchased at pharmacies or gas stations. It wasn't the drug of choice though for it was mainly labourers or truck drivers who used it. Ironically, after it became illegal, its price and popularity skyrocketed to the extent that it has become nothing short of a scourge on our youth. Last I heard the cost had more than tripled since before the ban.

A roadside vendor-cum-dealer on Sathon Soi 1 was the regular trading spot for people who were in the know. Sathon is the main business centre of Bangkok and not an area many would associate with drug dealing.

I'd always travel by taxi to do my deals. When the taxi arrived at the agreed spot, I'd lower the passenger window, raise my hand and nod. The person I was meeting would then approach and enquire how much I wanted and then promptly return with the goods. On one occasion, such a deal netted me an extra 5,000 baht, on top of my usual fee for sex.

The 'messiest' service I ever provided for a fee was during a New Year celebration in Pattaya. A *farang* bought a slew of boys from a go-go bar. The deal was that each boy would be paid 2,000 baht to ejaculate into his mouth in the privacy of his hotel room. Word got round to nearby bars and many extras had turned up on the appointed night. The *farang* awaited his semen 'shower' dressed in a very lavish suit. Ten boys would enter at a time while the others waited in the lobby. You would think that huddles of young men loitering in a hotel lobby would have aroused suspicion, but nobody said anything. The whole thing felt a little ridiculous, but I saw it as easy money. I usually had to perform a song and dance for the same amount at the bar. We joked that this experience of group masturbation was like the seasonal kite-flying contests we'd have as kids. The only difference was that those contests involved real kites .

Not all of the boys were able to perform though. Some were struck by stage fright and so forfeited their fee.

Still in the bathroom pondering all I had done for money in the past, I concluded that I'd participated in some very odd, dirty, and frequently illegal situations, so the prospect of smearing someone with faeces wouldn't really be that outlandish. Besides, I desperately needed the money. So that was it. The decision was made.

The studio, a townhouse in disguise, was in Nonthaburi, a province that adjoins Bangkok, but in reality is more like a suburb of the city. From the outside, our workplace looked very innocent indeed, and no one would've suspected what was really going on inside. Erik had already warned the cast and crew to keep their mouths shut about what we were up to.

I didn't feel particularly nervous making dirty porn. I quashed any rumblings of guilt by reminding myself that I was being well paid. Several other men were also acting in the films and all seemed to have adopted the same attitude. Our female co-stars had been recruited from bars in Nana. I scanned the room and saw many of them were obviously past their prime as prostitutes, whereas the few younger members were clearly desperate for money. Before shooting, the cast was required to test negative for STDs and AIDS. I later learned that Wan, Erik's wife, used to work in a Thaniya bar and had married a Japanese client. They later divorced though, and she married Erik. She obviously played a pivotal role in recruiting the women, negotiating prices, and so on.

Once we were assembled, we were given our individual roles and told who would be our partners. Once my partners had a face, the thought of committing unspeakable acts against them became all the more real and alarming. So I *wai*'d the woman, apologising in advance for what I was about to do. They all seemed resigned to their fates, however, and barely acknowledged my humble requests for forgiveness.

In some scenes, the women would smear my faeces all over their bodies pretending to like it. But, the most horrible shot by far involved me tying up and stripping my co-star. I then proceeded to smear her face, body and hair with the same matter. I wore gloves of course, but the smell was ghastly and I came close to vomiting on several occasions. These scenes went on for ages, shooting and re-shooting from every angle imaginable. As soon as a scene was over the women would run for the showers and scrub themselves raw.

A dog also shared one of the lead roles. He was injected with a stimulant that made him sexually excited and also very aggressive. The shoot was completed by an act of bestiality. The dog occasionally got carried away though, and even bit a few girls.

Some of the mellower scenes involved me having sex with three women, or ejaculating into a woman's mouth. The women were paid between 20,000 and 30,000 baht each depending on how many scenes they featured in. I asked Erik why he didn't just make porn films featuring regular coupling. That type of movie, he said, was for good-looking actors who had beautiful bodies; this kind, on the other hand, was for our type.

None of the actors were happy to be engaging in such displays but we all had our reasons, and focusing on these helped us through them. My reason was the welfare of my family, and I suspected other actors had similar motivations.

I worked for Erik intermittently for almost a year and have no idea how many movies in total I starred in. Wan and Erik even performed in some of the scenes themselves. I managed to keep my job a secret the entire time, especially from Thomas. I didn't contact anyone participating in these films after I left: enough was enough. Not only had the work been awful, but it also was extremely monotonous.

Had I been in those women's shoes, I'd never have let anyone do such demeaning things to me. Then again, I shouldn't have been the one doing it to them.

It's very hard for me to confess to any of this, but I need to unburden myself. I have to make amends for the life I've led. After all, being in hospital, I have had to let go of all remaining shreds of dignity. The nurses change my bedpan daily; I am almost naked, and my body is covered in dark, ugly welts. How could I possibly consider myself superior to the actresses in those movies now? I am suffering for the bad deeds of my past. I'm not even sure if they should feature in this book, but I can't turn back the clock. I can't undo what I've done; I can only compensate for it with honesty. So while we are on the topic I would like to clearly state that not every Thai would stoop to such low levels for money, not even those who work in the sex industry. Many people decided against working for Erik when they found out what would be involved. Of course, I would walk away if I was ever asked to do such things again. There are good and bad people in every society irrespective of how civilised any of them purport to be. The fact is that Erik exploited the women in his movies—he used their desperation to line his pockets.

Just as my patience with Thomas was beginning to wear thin, I found another patron—or rather, he found me. He turned out to be one of the kindest and most generous people I've ever met.

I was dancing on the stage one night when I noticed a smart-looking man staring at me. I thought he was Thai, but when I later introduced myself I discovered he was Chinese. He introduced himself as Lau, a Taiwanese hailing from Tainan City. I generally attracted *farang* men so was surprised when Lau expressed an interest in me. He was slim, fair-skinned, and his mid-length hair was stylish. He had movie-star looks, which would've driven Thai women crazy, and he didn't project a gay attitude at all. Unlike my usual clients, he was my age, and stood almost six feet tall, which is unusual for an Asian man. I boldly told him I liked him very much and wanted to go out with him. He immediately agreed, and without further ado we left for his office/apartment in Ratchadaphisek.

From that night on, Lau became my long-term benefactor and dearest friend. Of course, when I later moved in with him I was careful not to mention Nuan, let alone my son. Having netted such a wonderful catch, I promptly deserted the miserly Thomas. Nuan and Chuan continued to live in the room I rented for them and I visited them often.

In time, I discovered that Lau had his own patron/lover—a fellow countryman and a very wealthy businessman named Wu. The plot of our little love triangle was full of intrigue and deception. Wu covered up his illicit affair with Lau by hiring him as a manager to oversee the automobile-part factories he owned in Thailand. In a way, Lau and I were holding down similar jobs, but over all, Lau definitely took a higher road in life. Wu sent his lover overseas so that he could enjoy his little secret whenever he felt like it, without the threat of exposure.

Unlike me, Lau actually worked. He genuinely wanted Wu's enterprise to succeed and he employed four Thais to help him. I met Wu during one of his trips to check on the business and, of course, his lover. He was similar to me in stature, but was a little overweight and had thinning hair. But what he lacked in looks he made up for in style as he drove around in his sleek Porsche. He'd made a fortune exporting car parts to dealers in the USA. Wu appeared to be a business mentor to Lau, and Lau, in turn, assumed the role of devoted and faithful employee. I was the only person privy to the true nature of their relationship. Wu had no idea I was involved with Lau; he thought I was merely a local worker.

Lau didn't love Wu but he couldn't resist the luxuries and comforts that came with the relationship. Except for the fact that I was attracted to Lau, my feelings for him followed the same pattern. Aside from covering my daily expenses, Lau paid me a handsome allowance of 50,000 baht a month. I could only imagine how much Wu paid him. Lau was a wonderful person and a great companion but I couldn't commit to him as a full-time lover—my heart just wasn't in it. I didn't tell him my true feelings because I needed his money, so I silently continued to play the game just as he did with Wu. I asked him why he liked me so much—I was no longer the youthful go-go boy, and there were countless other good-looking gay boys who would've worshipped Lau if given the chance. He could have had anyone he wanted. Lau assured me that he didn't want anyone else—I was his type and he loved me. I'd believed beauty was one of the most desired qualities a person could possess—more than goodness even, and I'd often neglected the inside in favour of bettering the outside. So Lau amazed me by his answer.

Lau lavished both time and attention on me and was a faithful lover. My lack of self-esteem prevented me from realising that Lau considered me his equal. I wasn't just a boy toy to be discarded when a new-and-improved model came along. In many ways, I felt undeserving of such respect and affection. Yet I freely took his goodies without any qualms. When mobile phones were still uncommon in Thailand he bought me a latest high-tech one from Taiwan. I rushed straight to the bar, holding the phone aloft like a trophy for all the other go-go boys to admire.

I regularly found ways to go see Nuan and Chuan and figured that sooner or later Lau would start asking questions. I pre-empted a nasty situation and told him Nuan was my cousin, having been abandoned by her husband during her pregnancy. She'd been left to raise their small child on her own so I asked Lau to show kindness towards them by paying the rent on her room and he gladly agreed. When I introduced Nuan to Lau they got along very well and, as I'd hoped, Lau asked them to come live with us. This made life a lot easier for me, as it meant I no longer had to travel back and forth between Lau's apartment and the room in Bonkai.

In Lau's presence, I acted the role of Nuan's older cousin. But unbeknownst to him, I regularly slept with her. Nuan, on the other hand, was a willing accomplice in our charade. It's hard to believe that Lau never once questioned the true nature of my relationship with Nuan—perhaps he suspected something, but was happy to act dumb by playing along. I'd again promised Nuan I'd find an alternative job before Chuan was old enough to understand what I did for a living. So I asked Lau for money to open up a clothing stall. Nuan and I travelled to Prathunam together to buy wholesale T-shirts, which would then be sold on to tourists at marked-up prices. We set up a makeshift stall near the Surawong end of Patpong and were initially making a profit of about 1,000-2,000 baht a day. We opened early in the evening and worked late into the night when the tourists came out to play. Nuan was very happy to mind the stall; she brought Chuan with her, and he would sleep on a small makeshift bed while she worked. She was thrilled, as she'd always dreamed of running her own business. We earned a nice profit and were happy with our success. When she wasn't working at the stall, Nuan cleaned Lau's apartment and took care of other household duties. Lau thought of Nuan as both a friend and a housemaid. We were a happy bunch indeed.

Unfortunately, as the pressure of providing for my family eased, my big-headedness grew. Greed got the better of me once again as I'd found a goose whose golden eggs both lined my pocket and fed my ego. I always had ten thousand baht on me at any given time and stupidly, I thought I could easily double it through gambling. I wasn't worried that gambling is a crime in Thailand for, at the time, gambling houses weren't raided very often. The owners paid huge kickbacks every month to local police, which was enough to persuade the law to turn a blind eye.

During my first few ventures into gambling dens, I miraculously managed to come away with an extraordinary profit. I even shared some of my winnings with Lau as a way of thanking him. I was sure he'd be happy, but instead he warned me gravely against returning to the dens. He thought that in the long run they would bring only misery. I didn't listen and, as if cursed by his disapproval, started on a losing streak that continued from that day on. I returned home nightly to be greeted by Lau's disappointed looks, leaving me feeling more frustrated. Some nights I would lose everything and even accrue debt, which meant that I'd have to call Lau to bail me out. When my debts began to accumulate, I ransacked the apartment, stole as many valuables as I could carry and headed to a pawnshop. I took mobile phones, digital cameras, and other valuables that added up to large amount of money.

Lau must have been shocked—even appalled, when he realised what I'd done, but oddly enough he never confronted me. He spoke to Nuan instead. One day, she caught me red-handed putting Lau's mobile phone in my pocket and ordered me to put it back immediately. She then commented that she hadn't seen me using the mobile phone Lau had given me in quite a long time. I gave her a feeble excuse about loaning it to a friend and that I was only borrowing Lau's for the time being. She didn't believe me. So she searched my wallet and found a receipt from the pawnshop that proved I'd actually pawned the phone a week earlier. Nuan was furious and warned me not to mess things up when we were doing so well. She reminded me that I should be grateful to have a generous patron like Lau and not take him for granted. Instead of feeling ashamed at this rebuke, I just became angry. She'd been giving out to me a lot lately about all kinds of issues so I simply ignored her protests. I put Lau's phone back in my pocket and cursed her on my way out the door. She warned Lau against storing valuables in the house and ridiculed me in front of him by asking if I had the nerve to carry the refrigerator to the pawnshop. I felt as if they were ganging up on me and I hated it.

The fact that Nuan had a close ally in Lau made her more assertive and confrontational with me. So my response was to drink and gamble all the more. It was easy to do so when I didn't have to worry about making ends meet—Lau took care of that. Nuan and I began arguing frequently and my anger at her began to escalate into violence. I felt that I'd always been a good provider and that she shouldn't begrudge me a few pleasures. I was simply blind to the fact that it was actually Lau who was the provider now and not me. Once again in my life, I felt my masculinity slipping away.

CHAPTER 12

While still living with Lau, I met a couple from Hong Kong. They asked me to call them by their English names, Tony and Anna. The second they entered the bar, I was struck by Anna's beauty. At first glance, her eyes gave me the impression that she was timid; but a closer look revealed that there were flames of unfulfilled desire burning brightly behind the shy veneer. When her pouty lips broke into a smile, the room would light up. So I immediately set about catching her attention. Not only did I want to boast about her to my fellow go-go boys, but I also wanted to take revenge on Nuan. I felt emasculated by her constant nagging and thought that by sleeping with Anna I could reassert my masculinity.

I removed my underwear, stroked my penis until it became hard, and then used a tied condom to engorge it further. As I began dancing, I positioned myself near Tony and Anna in an effort to make eye contact with her. She smiled shyly as I gyrated my body in order to tantalise her. She lent over and whispered something to Tony, her overweight, middle-aged husband. Patience was my trump card. I waited until I was sure that I'd secured Anna's interest before approaching Tony. I figured they were no different from any of the other couples I'd encountered—another husband looking for a bar boy to pleasure his wife. We made small talk for a few minutes and then I was pleasantly surprised when Tony tipped me 500 baht. I'd done next to nothing to earn such a generous handout.

He then lent towards me and said, 'Tomorrow we come back and go enjoy? You massage?'

I assured him I did, knowing full well what he was implying. I could tell it was their first time hiring an additional lover, and I presumed they were buying themselves some time to talk about it before making a definite decision. I hoped they'd return, but suspected they might change their mind. True to their word though, they returned the following night. So I approached them with a big smile and *wai*.

Tony wasted no time. 'Everything okay? Can you go with us? You go give me and my wife massage?'

Anna gave me a sheepish smile from behind Tony's back. We all knew that a massage was the very least they were expecting from me.

I invited them into the bar and we sat down on a sofa, with me awkwardly seated between them. I assumed I'd need to help them relax a little before the night's activities began, but was taken by surprise when Anna's hand crept into my skimpy underwear and began playing with my penis. Meanwhile, Tony looked on approvingly. I knew then that I'd definitely be having sex with Anna. I'd never slept with such a beautiful Chinese lady but had always fantasised about it. Now

I was about to fulfil this fantasy and even get paid for it. Had I met Anna outside of the bar, I'd gladly have paid her to sleep with me. Not all Asian women appeal to me—especially if they are stubby, short-legged, and have no bottom. On the other hand, I adore Western women, who I find sexy, open, and most importantly, they treat me as an equal. I would gladly sleep with them for free. Anna was just as appealing, if not more so, than the white girls I fantasised about. I couldn't believe my luck that night in the bar.

When we arrived at their room we got straight down to business. Tony asked if I'd like to take a shower first and I hastily agreed. Anna did likewise. Tony was the last to wash up. Before he went into the bathroom he turned to me and said, 'You massage my wife now?' I began to slowly massage her as Tony exited the room. Anna was face-down on the bed as I lathered my hands in oil and began slowly kneading the muscles in her shoulders, back and buttocks, while blowing gently on her delicate skin. She spread her legs, allowing me to slip my hands between the cheeks of her buttocks. I eased my fingertips into her vagina and began slowly stimulating her. She was already moist, so I gently turned her over and began to run my tongue and hands all over her body. Not one inch of her gorgeous silken torso was left wanting, including her musky-scented nether region. She purred with pleasure as I began pleasing her with my tongue and fingers when Tony came from the shower. He walked over to the nightstand and retrieved a condom. After handing it to me he commanded, 'Make her happy.' I slid the condom on and entered her with a glorious thrust.

Anna cried out loudly as her whole body shuddered with pleasure. I continued ecstatically as she murmured something to Tony who translated that I was doing a great job. I'd been thrusting into her for some time before Tony helped us change positions. I stood up and Anna wrapped her legs and arms around me while Tony supported her back. He kissed and caressed her while I continued to pleasure her. Anna's eyes remained closed the entire time, as if she was lost in some erotic reverie. Sweat formed on her face as she rasped and bit her bottom lip sensually.

We climaxed simultaneously then collapsed on the bed, exhausted but deeply satisfied. No one was as content as me though. In a normal everyday scenario, I'd probably be killed for having sex with someone's wife, but here I'd been encouraged to do so . . . and was even paid for it. Life as a go-go boy is strange indeed.

I wanted to stay on and please them further, but the party was over. Tony picked up his wallet and counted out five one-thousand baht notes. Less than an hour had passed since I'd first stimulated Anna. In jest I kissed the bank notes, feeling like the luckiest man on earth. Before I excused myself, Tony turned to me and said, 'You come back here at 5pm tomorrow.'

I was overjoyed. Not only had I just been paid for sleeping with a beautiful woman, but I was being invited to do it all over again. This kind of rendezvous was to continue throughout their stay in Bangkok.

When the time came for Tony and Anna to fly home to their three children, Tony gave me his mobile number so we could meet up next time they came to Bangkok. They seemed content with my services. Tony told me he was willing to do anything to make Anna happy. Judging by the size of Tony's manhood, sexual pleasure was something he wasn't quite able to provide for her. Tony and Anna were the first two clients I ever really looked forward to encountering again. Each time we slept together, I wanted to win Anna over with my performance. I pulled out all the stops. I thought that I was a valued member of our love triangle, but in reality they probably thought of me as little more than a sex toy, a walking dildo if you will. For once Anna had climaxed, she didn't want anything to do with me.

While I was obsessing over ways of repaying my gambling debts, I received terrible news. My mother called imploring me to come home because Pa had gone missing. He'd left to go on business to a nearby town and hadn't been seen since. Mae feared the worst. The neighbours had formed a search party but, so far, their efforts had been fruitless. Mae feared Pa might have been drunk and fallen into a pond and drowned.

A few months beforehand, my father informed me of his plan to demand compensation from a man named Phisanu, who was the father of the boy who'd been driving the scooter when Choke was killed. We'd had a simple funeral for Choke and I thought that everyone had moved on by putting his untimely death behind them. But my father had continued to obsess over the details of the crash, and insisted our family was owed compensation. Suwan, the man who'd been teaching his wife to drive the pick-up truck that fateful night, offered my father 100,000 baht in compensation if he agreed not to press charges against him. Suwan was a teacher at the same school as my father and they'd actually been good friends. I don't know what my father was thinking—perhaps he felt some sort of loyalty to Suwan for old time's sake—but he accepted the money and dropped the charges.

The two boys who'd been on the scooter with my brother only incurred some minor bruising and a few fractures, so Suwan refused to pay them any compensation. So Phisanu, the father of the driver, demanded justice. He took his grievances to court in the hopes that he and the family of the other boy would be awarded compensation. In court, the two survivors insisted that my brother had been driving when the accident occurred. Meanwhile, Suwan insisted he'd seen Phisanu's son driving the vehicle. Instead of being awarded compensation, the court ruled that the driver, Phisanu's son, was guilty of reckless manslaughter and was sent to prison. The court case had backfired on all involved. Phisanu was devastated by the verdict and cursed my father ever since. A series of brawls and angry outbursts ensued.

Rather than letting bygones be bygones, my father's lawyer suggested Pa seek compensation from

Phisanu also, since his son had been found guilty of manslaughter. I don't think my father's motives were purely mercenary though. Phisanu had publicly disgraced him with vitriolic attacks on his character, and my father's pride had been deeply wounded. So he insisted Phisanu pay up. His incessant demands for compensation served only to worsen the rift between them. Phisanu threatened my father with all kinds of violence but Pa thought he was merely putting on a show of false bravado. It was a shame that relations had soured between them; once our two families were extremely close. Both sides had lost loved ones in the accident and, rather than causing them to bond over their shared grief, it only drove a wedge between them. I pleaded with my father to let it go, but between his macho pride and desperation to save face, he refused to listen.

We Thais believe that when it's someone's time to go back to their old home—that is, to die—then it's impossible to change that destiny. That was the last conversation I had with my 62-year-old father.

By the time I arrived at the village, my father's body had been found. He'd been dead for four days. They discovered him face down on the roadside. I was the only member of my family called to identify the body, yet I barely recognised him. The Khmer tattoo on his back was the only identifiable feature that revealed the corpse to be that of my father. He was horribly bloated, and one of his ears had been almost completely torn off; his face was covered in dried blood and both his eyes sat unnaturally in their sockets. Wriggling maggots seemed to delight in destructively gorging his flesh—a sight that brought home to me the reality of what had actually happened. My father was dead. It was a soul-destroying moment. My stomach wrenched violently and I couldn't help but throw up. I cried out in agony, like a wounded animal. Words can never adequately explain what it was like seeing my father that way.

Ligature marks criss-crossed his body, suggesting rope had been used to restrain him. It was no accident that killed him; my father had been brutally murdered. My heart sank even further. I agonised thinking about how he'd struggled as his killers were beating him. I found it nearly impossible to come to grips with the horrific fate that had befallen my dearest Pa.

A policeman investigating the scene, who I later learned was a good friend of Phisanu's, tried to convince me my father's death had been accidental. He claimed my father had been the victim of a hit and run. Clearly, this made no sense. Had it been the case, the search party would have found him almost immediately since it would've happened in such an obvious spot. A hit and run didn't explain the rope marks and other horrific wounds all over his body. Pa had obviously been abducted, tied up, and beaten to death. His body had possibly been hidden in the forest for some days before the killers decided to later dump him on the roadside. I desperately wanted to believe my father's death hadn't been so barbaric; but the evidence stared us all in the face.

The inquest confirmed our fears. Pa had received repeated blows to his head and body from a blunt object. It'd been raining continuously for several days, making it impossible to gather any real evidence, so it was never revealed exactly where he'd been killed. I concluded that whoever did it, wasn't acting alone.

While my siblings and mother busied themselves preparing for Pa's funeral, I occupied myself with gathering information through the local rumour mill. Mae told me that Pa was supposed to be going on business for half a day but never returned. Sombat, an acquaintance of my father, said he'd asked Pa to join their usual evening drinking circle on the day he disappeared and Pa had apparently done so, before leaving the party in a drunken stupor. I became suspicious of Sombat. He was the last person to see my father alive and also happened to be the one to discover his body. Pa usually walked home from Sombat's along a small track which wove its way through an area of dense forest which, nonetheless, was inhabited by a handful of residents. At night-time though, the place was deathly quiet and a man's screams would surely have been heard. After much prodding on my part, one of the locals confessed that he and his family had heard a pick-up truck race down the small road on the night in question. They also heard the distinct cries of a man in trouble. But they thought a fight had broken out between local louts and decided that it'd be better not to get involved.

I slowly began to piece together the night's events as best I could. My father's attackers must have come after him in a pick-up truck and abducted him. They then took him to a secure location and tortured him to death, before surreptitiously dumping the body at an opportune time in order that it be found half a week later. Nobody was willing to give any other information so this fragmented picture was the best I could come up with.

The more I delved into the crime the more convinced I'd become that I would be next on the murderers' hit list. After all, I was nosing about and no doubt ruffling some feathers, especially judging by the nervous responses I was getting to my questions. I realised I needed to be more cautious when probing the locals. For all I knew, some of them might have been in cahoots with Phisanu, even helping to carry out the crime. Or if they hadn't been directly involved, they may have had knowledge that would have put them in danger if they decided to disclose it. The atmosphere was less than cooperative, and the more information I gathered, the more confused I became.

One thing I was certain about was that Phisanu was the mastermind. I confided this thought with a close friend who promptly informed me that for 20,000 baht he could put a hit on Phisanu. Another friend offered to sell me an M16 so I could take matters into my own hands. I drank countless bottles of rice whiskey but nothing drowned the anger and hatred simmering within me. The only thing that prevented me from taking the law into my own hands was the fact I had a son and wife to think of. I didn't want to perpetuate an endless cycle of revenge and death. If I avenged my father by killing Phisanu, it'd only be a matter of time before his family came after me. I reluctantly put the matter to rest, and prayed that karma would decide the fate of those responsible for Pa's death.

Pa's funeral had few attendants, which for me was further proof that many villagers had somehow been involved in his death, even if only by refusing to talk. They might have feared that Phisanu would interpret their attendance as disrespectful, or even as a way of pointing the finger at him. For others, I'm sure an uneasy conscience kept them away. I was enraged and threw all caution to the wind. I began accusing whoever I saw partying or merrymaking at the time of Pa's funeral. His so-called friends, who eagerly soaked up free booze and money at his expense for years, were nowhere to be seen. At the end of the day, despite his reputation for kindness, my father had very few real friends.

My mother still hadn't come to terms with Choke's death and the loss of my father crippled her. After the funeral, she began to complain of powerful headaches, which she believed were a sign Pa wanted her to follow him into the afterlife. She claimed he called to her softly in her dreams.

The police finally recorded my father's death as a murder; however, to this day, no arrests have been made.

I went back to Bangkok drained and defeated. It took me a long time to readjust, and to be honest, I never really did. I relied on my trusted friend, alcohol, to help me cope with the loss. Gambling also diverted my thoughts from the pain.

The last time I met my Hong Kong sweethearts, I brought my wife and son along to meet them at the airport. I lied again by saying Nuan was my cousin and Chuan my nephew. To thank us for welcoming them so hospitably, they treated us to a lavish dinner in an expensive restaurant. Nuan and Chuan then went home and I stayed on to take care of Anna, at Tony's insistence. After I'd pleasured Anna in the usual fashion, I brazenly asked her for 30,000 baht to help pay off my gambling debts. This was the first time Anna had ever heard anything of my addiction. Tony interjected that he didn't have that kind of cash and instructed me to come to see him the following day. They stopped taking my phone calls and abruptly vanished from their hotel room without a trace. I'd overstepped an invisible boundary and due to my greed, shot myself in the foot. I was not a charity case, so by stepping outside of my designated role they simply discarded me. I'd deluded myself, believing I had the upper hand in the relationship thinking they actually needed me and my sexual prowess. I felt that Tony's shortcomings in bed gave me licence to take advantage of them. I found out the hard way that Tony had the power all along. He hired me to be his wife's lover, but the moment I became too demanding he simply replaced me with someone else.

I might have been able to penetrate Anna's sex, but her bond with Tony was something I could never interfere with. I was hired help and nothing more.

A year after Pa died, my mother called me on a regular basis, begging me to help her organise a ritual called *riak kwan* at her house. This religious ceremony is supposed to help strengthen and secure the spirit and thus prevent its being robbed from the body. She believed Pa desperately wanted her to join him in the spirit world, and that through the strength of his desires, he somehow stole part of her spirit. She claimed that Pa's powerful yearnings were manifested in physical form by the mind-numbing headaches she was experiencing. I suggested that it was her negative thoughts causing the headaches and begged her to see a doctor. I swore she'd be able to heal herself if she followed my instructions.

In reality, I was terrified of returning to my village. I'd accused countless people of being involved in my father's murder and believed that they might come after me. When I learnt my mother had been hospitalised, I sent Nuan to care for her, rather than do so myself. Mae died in her sleep in a lonely hospital bed. She was 59.

The doctors told us afterwards that throughout the hours preceding her death she appeared to be incoherently talking to someone. Of course, no one was present. Lau generously gave me 20,000 baht to pay for her funeral.

I lost three family members within a short period of time and I was inconsolable with grief. I alternated between moods of depression and guilt. I wondered if my mother might have lived longer if I'd helped her carry out the *riak kwan* ritual as she'd asked. She'd suffered two great losses and her will to live just ebbed away. After Pa's death, Mae was all alone; one by one her children simply returned to their families. My mother's only companions had been the neighbours—many of whom we suspected had been involved in Pa's murder—and her relatives who visited rarely. I could've asked her to come live with us in Bangkok; instead, I selfishly stuck my head in the sand. I'd disappointed her so many times, and when I had a chance to make things right, I chose not to.

I have made many mistakes, but the wrongs I committed against my parents really are the actions I regret the most. I often worry that one day my own children will abandon me in the same manner. And if it does happen, I will have no choice but to accept it.

My life was collapsing around me like a house of cards. Losing a large part of my family in such a short space of time was too much to cope with. Each death brought its own tidal wave of sorrow, and my own will to live seemed to be drifting away.

Shortly after my mother's funeral, Wu discovered I was sleeping with Lau. I'm not sure how he found out, but I suspect he instructed one of Lau's workers to spy on the true nature of our relationship. Wu stopped sending

Lau's salary and thus the allowance I received from Lau was substantially reduced. Lau had no choice but to close up shop and return to Taiwan to make amends with Wu. Everything happened so quickly that I was left reeling in uncertainty. I was still up to my eyeballs in debt. The rent on the apartment was very expensive; so Nuan and I decided to pawn whatever furniture we could and move into a small room. My life was truly built on the shifting sand.

My dreams of buying a fancy car and house with Lau's money would never be realised. We were now worse off than when we had started out. I was older but, sadly, none the wiser. Had I listened to Lau's warnings, I might have escaped the clutches of addiction and emerged from our relationship financially secure. I was given an opportunity to better myself and I screwed up.

I should've stayed in touch with Lau, but I was too lazy. I mistreated him badly. It will take many lifetimes to make it up to him. I truly wish him all the best and hope he has found a man who loves him and treats him well.

Unfortunately, the abrupt termination of my relationship with Lau coincided with the bird flu epidemic in Thailand in early 2004. The tourist industry crashed and burned, taking with it our T-shirt stall. I returned to the go-go scene, but at 35 years of age I had passed the sell-by date and clients rarely bought me. The outlook was bleak. When punters did buy me, the *Mama-san* and bar captain would mockingly congratulate me with a standing ovation. I wanted to yell out how I once had been a top boy over whom *farangs* fought but there was no point in aggravating them and risking losing my job.

I could no longer move from bar to bar; my reputation as an unreliable alcoholic preceded me. Nobody wanted to invite trouble into their bars, so I was turned down at most places.

Nuan decided it'd make more economic sense for her to go back to work full-time while I minded our son. We'd become friendly with my sister Nit's husband, and Nuan asked him for a job. They'd established a successful grilled chicken/fresh fruit vendor in Prathunam. Although Nuan didn't get along well with my sister, she was willing to keep the peace in order to make some much-needed money.

Nuan and I had been together for four years and I reasoned that since I had been taking care of her so well, it was my turn to be 'kept' for a change. I considered myself open-minded enough to allow Nuan become the rice-winner. I whiled away the days by minding Chuan, and by drinking and gambling. But with Nuan holding the financial reins, I wasn't allocated much money for spending on the two latter activities. I'd stopped visiting gambling houses and instead threw my bets down with friends on games of chess and other frivolities, such as guessing the colour of panties a woman wore—don't ask me how we found out though.

Nuan hissed at me if I asked her for as little as 50 baht to spend on leisure pursuits. She rebuked me for drinking even a single can of beer, arguing that her hard-earned wages should be spent wisely on important necessities and not on profligate activities. She growled, 'You don't want to help row our family boat then at least keep your feet out of the water, and stop slowing us down!'

As our arguments became more heated, she became aloof. She resented me and our sex life petered to nothing. I tried to make things up to her by helping out in little ways. I accompanied her to the market to buy produce early every morning with a sleepy Chuan in tow. One day she asked me to hold Chuan, and then, as if to spite me, sat down beside a strange man as far away from me as possible. We'd had rough patches before, but she'd never acted this distant with me. It was as if the moment I'd ceased to be the wage earner, Nuan's love simply dried up.

Her attitude towards me slowly eroded my self-confidence. I'd been unceremoniously demoted as family head and felt I had to do something to reinstate myself. So I pulled a childish coup by venting my anger with senseless violence. I became irrational, and regularly attacked Nuan without provocation. Nuan fought back at first, but her resistance only inspired more violence.

She was eventually forced to develop and deploy survival skills. If she sensed danger brewing she'd quickly grab Chuan and flee the house until my anger abated. She later confessed that during the worst times she would mix sleeping pills into my rice to sedate me.

After each brutal bout, I'd have no recollection of what had transpired the previous night. Nuan would then sadly recount the events, describing my viciousness in excruciating detail.

My destructive behaviour got us kicked out of one rented room after another. In each new abode, it took no time for other tenants to begin complaining about the noise which invariably sent the landlord knocking. When sobriety and remorse eventually kicked in, I sincerely swore that I'd change. However, I was neither willing nor capable of parting with alcohol; for me, life without it was inconceivable.

The inevitable finally happened. Nuan came home one evening, exhausted from work, only to find me in yet another drunken stupor. She began lecturing me in the usual fashion, berating me as if I was a good-for-nothing burden. I responded with equal passion. Our raised voices caused Chuan to stir from his sleep, so Nuan opened the door and headed down the stairs. I was hot on her heels, my anger reaching boiling point.

'Bitch,' I shouted, 'if you want to leave me, go ahead. I'm clearly useless to you, but leave the boy with me.'

Nuan chucked softly.

'How on earth could a washed-up prostitute like you ever earn a living and support a child?'

I was stunned. Her words cut me to the heart. I felt I could kill her; but instead I spun on my heels and marched off in the direction of Soi Twilight. I needed a drink to calm myself and it didn't take long to find one.

While I was drowning my sorrows, Nuan packed her bags. Our relationship was sinking fast and she'd decided to jump ship before it was too late. I staggered home later that evening only to find an empty room. Chuan's milk bottles and tiny clothes had vanished into the night along with his mother. The reality of the situation sobered me instantly. Nuan hadn't even left a goodbye note. I broke down in tears and, not knowing how else to deal with grief, I trashed the room, destroying everything in sight. Hearing the racket, my neighbours rang the landlord. A short while later, two stout men came and 'kindly' escorted me off the premises.

CHAPTER 13

In the blink of an eye, I found myself homeless, wifeless, and childless. I only had the clothes on my back and a small amount of cash. Distraught, I questioned how Nuan could do such a thing? Who was she to cast judgement? She'd been a willing accomplice in every deception that had put food on the table for us. I'd taken care of her for years and couldn't understand her sudden change of attitude. I'd stupidly believed she'd put up with any treatment and would never have left me. But now she was suddenly make a living on her own. She didn't have to put up with my foolishness any longer.

She finally realised I wouldn't change and that I would eventually become an even greater burden to her. So she decided to put Chuan's needs first and bring him up in a safe and stable environment; an environment unpolluted by my presence.

As time went on I realised the clincher in our relationship had come a long time before that fateful night when she left. We'd been brawling as usual, when suddenly a look of horror washed over Nuan's face. Her mortified gaze was fixed somewhere behind me. Nuan pushed me aside with all her might.

I was furious that she'd dare use force on me and I was ready to exact punishment on her. I spun around and what greeted me caused me to freeze in my tracks. Chuan was holding a stick, waving it back and forth protectively with a fierce look of determination on his face. Realising I was about to hurt his mother, he'd sprung to her defence. He was only four years old. The sight of my boy brandishing a stick against me drained all the anger from me. Nuan, with tears in her eyes, carefully pried the weapon from his hands and held him tightly.

'Don't ever try to hurt your pa. Hurting your parents is one of the most serious sins a child can commit,' she told him. We quietly retreated to our respective corners, too shocked to say a word.

The following day Nuan shared her deep concerns that I might eventually hit Chuan while drunk. I saw red, 'I'm not the type of scum who would harm his own flesh and blood!' Ironically, I started pummelling her with my fists as I shouted this at her. I knew that she was right; there was no telling what I was capable of. I was powerless, and too proud to admit it.

After they left, my money soon ran out. I reluctantly decided to head to Soi Twilight, but not to work; rather, I did so to seek handouts from my buddies. The next few months passed in a drunken blur. I awoke many mornings in a crumpled, shirtless heap either on the floor of a bar in Soi Twilight or on the side of a road.

I reeked of alcohol, sweat, urine, and vomit. I looked awful as my hair was dirty, long, and dishevelled, and my face red and swollen.

On occasion, if I was both lucky and sober, I found a deserted bar bathroom in which I could wash up. Though when I say wash up, I mean give my underarms and face a quick scrub. If I was extremely fortunate, a bar manager would take pity and allow me to use the shower in his premises. For someone who'd once taken such pride in his appearance, what a contrast to be now spending my days as a dirty itinerant.

Even though I was living hand to mouth, I always found empty drink bottles next to me each morning. I couldn't remember where I'd gotten the money to buy them though. I imagine my acquaintances took pity on me and handed me a few baht which I promptly, of course, poured down my throat. I was desperate for alcohol and was prepared to do anything to procure it. A friend even dared me to run the gauntlet of the *soi* in my underwear for his entertainment. When he waved 100 baht in front of me I drunkenly obliged. Apparently, passers-by looked on in disgust as I careened up and down the street like a mad man dodging the vendors and tourists.

My bedraggled appearance caused strangers to whisper while staring at me. If I approached them for small change, they usually shooed me away as they would a diseased dog. They probably assumed I was a deranged lunatic who'd escaped an asylum or something. Even my own acquaintances questioned my sanity, suggesting the trauma of Nuan's departure caused me to lose my mind.

Once a tourist reported me to the police and I was arrested and detained in a holding cell for several days. The police were surprisingly reasonable with me and viewed me as a harmless drunk who was to be pitied rather than scorned. I *wai*'d them upon release, apologising for the commotion I'd caused.

On numerous occasions I found myself crouching on the curb trying to summon the courage to throw myself into oncoming traffic. I wanted to escape this horrible life as fast as possible, but was too cowardly even for this. Go-go dancing was no longer an option and I wasn't suitable for much else. The only motivation to get up in the morning was to scrape enough money together to purchase my cure-all medicine.

Silom Road is full of businessmen rushing about in their expensive suits. It's also home to the mentally ill, the homeless, amputee beggars, blind buskers, and hungry mothers and children looking for a few baht to put food in their bellies. These poor, unfortunate people contrast sharply with the yuppies and tourists jostling each other in the thoroughfare. Significantly, it was the former group who provided me with an important life lesson.

After finally reaching a bottom of sorts, I wallowed in the gutters, stewing over my problems, and realised that in comparison to these poor folk, I had nothing to complain about. I could see, and still had use of all my limbs. I could work, if I could only pull myself together emotionally that is. I decided it was time to get my life back; besides, my friends' charity had dried up, so I had to take charge. I began wandering the streets in search of dropped change. A 20-baht note had become a small fortune to me and I found myself doing something I'd never done in the past—I began saving money. I spent money only on what I needed rather than on things I simply wanted. Between gambling houses, brothels, and nightclubs, I'd blown a fortune. Now it was time for me to possess money, and not let it possess me. As my mindset slowly evolved, so did my behaviour, and acquaintances recognised that I was making a genuine effort to change. They offered me dishwashing or waiting jobs and I gratefully accepted them. I was winning them over slowly, and a friend even rented a small room for me. I'd begun to reassemble the pieces of my shattered life.

I discovered that Nuan was living with her friend in a small room behind Wat Hualamphong, a fifteen minute walk from Soi Twilight. Rumour had it that she'd found herself a new man. I hung around the area on a daily basis, hoping to 'accidentally' meet her. I thought I could beg her to return to me. Days turned into weeks and there was still no sign of her and I began to lose hope. I eventually summoned the courage to knock on Nuan's door only to be greeted by her girlfriend. She emphatically insisted Nuan had moved out of the soi the moment she heard I was looking for her and hadn't left an address. I'd fought hard to get as far as I had, so I decided to let go of Nuan and move on. I wasn't going to let regrets pull me down as they had in the past.

Often, when one door closes, another one opens. That's exactly what happened in my case. The very same evening I gave up on Nuan, I met two beautiful ladies at a bar in Soi Patpong 2. I could tell from their dresses and seductive manner that they were prostitutes. Aside from the obvious sexiness and sultry good looks, something else drew me to them. They happened to be chatting away in my childhood language, Khmer. Their accents revealed that they were from one of the Isan provinces bordering Cambodia. In a bold move, I marched up to them and greeted them warmly in our mother tongue. The two ladies were impressed and urged me to join them for a drink. Sao, the prettier of the two, motioned me to sit next to her. A spark ignited between us as we chatted about our lives and common backgrounds.

From the start, Sao was upfront about being an experienced lover. I was hoping things would move fast between us, but even I was surprised by the lightening speed at which she boldly groped and kissed me. I'd longed for a woman's touch for months and was overjoyed she'd made a move on me. We managed to control our desires long enough to make our way to my decrepit room.

Sao was indeed a great lover. I was in heaven. We were marooned sex workers who'd found an island of refuge in each other. After my experience with Ple in Pattaya, I never again entertained the thought of going out seriously with a working girl. I considered them 'indecent' because they slept with 'thousands' of men. Of all people though, I should've been able to empathise with their situation.

It was our common backgrounds that helped us to bond quickly, along with a shared love for drink and partying. Being as lonely as I was, she moved in with me without hesitation. With her arrival came the habits I'd diligently avoided in the past months—I traded an empty bed for another round of problems which were to surface later on.

Despite her beauty, as a prostitute, Sao was also in her twilight years. Our bodies were no longer attractive enough to work as go-go dancers, so we were forced to find alternative forms of employment. We therefore agreed to perform together in a nightclub sex show.

Every evening, tour groups of Asians and Europeans —both male and female—arrived at the club. They filed noisily out of coaches, not knowing what to expect from the evening's activities.

I would start off the entertainment by mingling with the crowd in my G-string and ladies giggled at the sight of my exposed behind. I wasn't as confident as I'd once been, but tried not to let my insecurities prevent me from doing my job. There were a total of three male performers, me included. We knew each other well since we were all ex-go-go boys whose paths had crossed many times over the years. Before we took to the stage, it was the girls who would warm up the audience by walking amongst them in either bikinis or their birthday suits.

Suddenly, with great fanfare, the music dramatically sounded and the lights dimmed. Sao and I took to the stage and began our ritualistic lovemaking. I slathered her with oil, paying special attention to her breasts and buttocks. As we ground our bodies against each other demonstratively, our hands continued on a frantic search for each other's 'pleasure'. We culminated our act with loud screams as I banged my penis into her from behind—each thrust making a loud smacking sound on her oil sodden bottom. I was loyal to Sao, and never penetrated anyone else during these shows, even though I performed simulated sex upon the other women.

Some of the shows involved women using their vaginas to shoot ping-pong balls into the air while customers lobbed them back with bats provided by the club. These women even used their sex organs to open bottles of soft drink and expertly shoot darts at targets. The most elaborate trick I ever witnessed involved a woman turning water into coke. She began by inserting a bottle of water into her vagina and proceeded to empty it of its contents. She displayed the empty bottle to the audience, then reinserted the bottle and filled it with brown fluid, which she proudly showed to the audience as Coke. No matter how much I coaxed them, the girls wouldn't reveal their secret. The only explanation I could come up with was that they'd placed some kind of coloured powder inside of them which mixed with the water to make it look like 'Coke'.

On Soi Patpong, many bars are on the ground floor and passers-by can sneak a free glimpse of bikini-clad women dancing around poles. Sex shows and other risqué attractions are generally confined to the upper floors. Before the so-called social moral reformation, there were fewer restrictions on nudity in these bars. Girls were allowed to dance topless or use pasties or tassels to cover their nipples.

The nightclub Sao and I worked in was near Rama IV intersection. I suspected the bar owner had a special deal with several tour guides because there was never any shortage of customers. Sao and I agreed that we were okay with each other soliciting for sex. It was only work so there was no need to be jealous. Our chief concern was making money, especially now that we were older.

The nightclub we worked in made a fortune charging each patron 1,000 baht per drink. The tour guide, on the other hand, earned a whopping 10,000 baht for every group of tourists they brought with them. It seemed there was never a shortage of money in the club, so it was a good place for us to work.

My relationship with Sao was fine and I believed my life held a degree of security. Just when things were looking up though, Sao got into a fight with the manager which heralded the end of our employment. She'd been taken by a client several days in a row, earning the nightclub 6,000 baht in bar fines, of which she received only 600 baht. She felt she deserved a larger percentage but the management disagreed. She quit, and I was left with little alternative but to follow—without her I didn't have an act.

The struggle to make a living after that never ceased. We both tried to sell our bodies whenever and wherever we could. We even tried to entice customers into bars and then request a commission from the management. The bar world had changed dramatically over the years and Sao and I were floundering and out of touch in many ways.

Nowadays, male sex workers in the Silom area punch their cards before 8pm if they want to collect a 100-baht bonus. The other staff, such as doormen, waiters, cashiers, DJs and bartenders, must show up before 6pm in order to clean the bar and make sure everything's in order for the night ahead. The dancers change into work underwear, and the gay and *kathoey* boys apply make-up to pretty themselves up. Each boy is assigned a number tag which is clipped on the front of their underwear so that clients can easily identify who they'd like to buy. A rotation system ensures fresh faces are constantly taking to the stage: with each change of song a new boy steps up to replace a fellow exiting. The go-go boys dance, strut, and prance, trying to catch the eye of a client. It's a merry-go-round of boys for sale. The boys' crotch area happens to be located exactly at the audience's eye level —a shrewd feature worked into the design of the stage and seating area.

The foreign female clients are the ultimate trophies— they guarantee pleasure, money, and face amongst our crew of dancers who are often jealous when anyone else bags a whitey. The one perk I've had from sex work is the opportunity to sleep with women from many backgrounds: Korean, Japanese, Chinese, Indian, white, and black—you name it, I've done it! Having so many multicultural notches on my bedpost is a macho reward indeed.

I encountered one sexually uninhibited black woman whom I shall never forget. She was extremely beautiful, with dark smooth skin, almond eyes, and a tall, lean, muscular body. She wasn't timid at all, and bought me and a gay co-worker for a night of fun and games. It was an orgiastic event that found us woven together in as many positions as can be imagined. Finally she pleasured my co-worker orally while I penetrated her from behind. Her plumbing was rather roomy though, and I was unable to satisfy her with my penis alone, so I masturbated her clitoris while simultaneously satisfying myself inside her. She was a constant stream of energy and excitement and came to a roaring climax, writhing and screaming uncontrollably, the likes of which I'd never seen in anyone before or since. The sheets were soaked with her juices and both us boys were exhausted.

When a white woman looked as if she might purchase me, I became particularly excited and had to remind myself not to appear too giddy in case I blew my chances. While making love, I liked assuring them of their beauty which always seemed to be appreciated. I often fantasised of having a child together and even told them as much; though this never went over as well as the comments on their good looks.

The funny thing is, we Thais used to consider Eurasian children to be *kaya songkhram*, or 'war trash'— in other words, they were the leftovers from Western soldiers after they had pulled out of the Vietnam War. Over the years, attitudes have changed, and it's now considered 'fashionable' to have a mixed child. Many *luk khruengs*, or 'half-half children', have succeeded in show business or modelling because of their exotic looks. Black-Thai children used to be subjected to great ridicule, especially if they didn't know who their GI fathers were, but, a decade or so after the war, when they became teenagers, all that changed. The Sports Authority of Thailand began head-hunting these same children, grooming them to become sports stars because they had stronger bodies and greater stamina.

Sleeping with white women also served as a soothing balm to my fractured ego. I adored the fact that they took charge about what they wanted from me. Unlike female Thai clients, I found white women daring and uninhibited. I recently read a survey which claimed that 70% of Thai women have never had an orgasm. This statistic was attributed to the fact that Thai men are purportedly the world's least satisfying lovers. I can't help but wonder why these women didn't go ahead and please themselves if their men were incapable of doing so. Or at the very least demonstrate to their lovers what they like in bed? In my opinion, they have no one to blame but themselves.

The boys take to the stage at 8.30pm, dancing for the first hour and a half before the sex shows begin. These shows include all sorts of complicated acrobatic moves—which involved our bouncing on top of one another while twisting and turning and penetrating each other. The performers are required to have great stamina and poise. In the past, go-go boys were required to reach orgasm and, moreover, to prove it; but this is no longer the case, although some bars still advertise ejaculation as a selling point to draw customers. On special occasions, the manager of go-go bars will host ladyboy or male beauty contests. These events always pull good crowds, especially amongst the bar boys themselves as well as among the gay and *kathoey* community.

From my own experience, *farang* bar owners are usually nicer to their boys than their Thai competitors. They don't view their employees as mere machines to discard once broken down. A *farang* boss has been known to rent rooms for his boys after they became infected with HIV, in some cases even giving their wives and children allowances and covering medical expenses.

Over the past decade, a growing number of university students have turned to the sex industry to fund their studies. Some need money simply because their parents are unable to support them. Others turn to the sex industry because they feel pressured by peers to buy brand-name goods and expensive digital gadgets to earn face. Some women only sell themselves so they can purchase handbags and designer clothes in order to look attractive and hopefully get the attention of a long-term lover or patron.

One of the main reasons for male students' selling their bodies is that they've incurred huge debts from gambling on European football matches. This kind of gambling is done through an agent called *a to*, meaning 'a table'. The bets are placed over a mobile phone or on the Internet so that the police can't track them. If the students lose, they're obliged to cough up the money fast or else face the wrath of hired thugs who tend to balance the books in their own unique manner. Therefore, the easiest way of making quick money is simply by putting their family jewels up for sale. Most working boys in bars—be they straight, gay or *kathoey*—generally get along. There are some nasty fistfights in gay town from time to time, but the catfights amongst the girls of Patpong are more frequent. It's hard to gauge what percentage of go-go boys in Soi Twilight are straight, gay, or bisexual. I know of one bar that claims to hire only straight men, yet I've seen many of the bar's clients walking out with petite, gay boys.

In my experience, straight men seem to be bolder and less inhibited about taking their underwear off or fondling their privates on stage. Ironically, gay and *kathoey* go-go boys are more reserved in this regard. I've always identified myself as straight both inside and outside of the workplace. I've experienced rare moments of joy during my time working in the sex industry but mostly, it's not exactly been fun. I don't know how gay and *kathoey* co-workers feel about their job—nobody wants to admit that they hate their careers and thus that they're living a lie. The one difference between me and my gay/*kathoey* counterparts is that they can be optimistic about the possibility of finding a long-term client or even developing a relationship beyond that of punter and prostitute.

Some bars divide their boys into two groups according to the perceived tastes of Western and Asian gay clients. *Farangs* generally go for well-built dark-skinned boys, while Asians prefer the slim and lighter-complexioned kind. However, there's no single formula when it comes to the rules of attraction.

These days, there's less stigma associated with being a sex worker than in the past. Success and wealth are highly regarded by family and friends, wherever the source of it may be. In rural areas, parents will brag about the amount of money their children send home each month. Competition amongst neighbouring families can be fierce.

These same parents prefer not to acknowledge that their sons and daughters sell their bodies to finance a new TV or motorcycle. They pretend their offspring work in nice offices or fancy restaurants. It's as if money absolves one of all sins, wiping the slate clean of any indecencies committed in the acquisition of it. It's hard to eradicate this type of thinking when poverty is widespread and wealth is the only means of garnering respect. Suddenly, neighbours are eager to socialise with the nouveau riche, being no longer considered destitute village vermin. Of course, not all villagers have such a mindset, but it is still the mindset that is most prevalent. I admire those who succeed in resisting this way of thinking though, and put the welfare of their children above any materialistic outlook. However, trading a child for wealth and benefits is something that's not only carried out by the poor. Many marriages among the elite in high society are arranged on the premise that such unions would be good for the family name and/or future business success; in my opinion, it's merely a higher and classier form of prostitution.

It is considered shameful to return to one's village with no evidence suggesting one has gone from rags to riches. The first question on everyone's lips is, 'How much money do you make in Bangkok?' If your answer is hundreds of thousand of baht per year you'll be praised. If you divulge that you're making next to nothing or worse yet, are unemployed, they'll likely walk away uninterested. Some factory workers dread going home because fellow villagers expect them to throw lavish celebrations, showering them with gifts. Those who do return to their families during annual festivals often find themselves incurring debt while trying to maintain face with their greedy neighbours.

I'm not saying that selling one's body is the worst career in the world—it's my body after all and I'm free to do whatever I want with it. All workplaces have pros and cons, and dos and don'ts; the go-go bars are no exception.

Mama-sans act as the middlemen: they greet clients at the door, escort them to their seats, sit with them, make small talk, and then help choose a boy who best fits their 'spec'. I quickly learned that it was important to maintain good relationships with *Mama-sans;* otherwise they'll recommend the boys they favour most over you. Worse yet, they may badmouth you, rendering you unsaleable. Working in the industry exposes one to copious amounts of alcohol, gambling, and drugs, and it is hard to resist these temptations. There are three golden rules that every go-go boy must abide by on a bar's premises—no gambling; obedience to the boss; and no drug taking. Yet drugs are freely available and addiction is rife—with some boys even dying or losing their minds in the process. Sadly, many former go-go boys resort to small-time theft when they can't sell themselves.

I strongly recommend that sex tourists not employ the services of streetwalkers, as the chances of being drugged and robbed, or worse, are considerably high. Downtown Bangkok is home to ladyboys who are famous for their snatch-and-run and undetectable pickpocket tactics.

Staying in this industry too long, however, can easily make one resent having to work for 'clean' money. Not that what we do doesn't count as work—it certainly does—however, most go-go boys wouldn't be able to tolerate a nine-to-five job with a boss constantly breathing down their necks, especially after living what they consider to be a free life. Like me, many go-go boys squander their money and before they know it, their lifestyle has chewed them up and spat them out. As you mature, even if you can master your money, you can't find work very easily to earn it. A younger generation of go-go boys are nipping at your heels and taking first pick of the clients. The attractive, successful boys usually disappear from the *soi* pretty quickly – they usually secure a lifelong patron who buys them a house, or they start a business with their generous earnings. Some of my former co-workers became bar managers while others had real business acumen and ended up owning bars.

In my opinion, aging *farang* men forming relationships with younger Thai partners is a grey area. I don't feel that one party is taking advantage of the other. The older partners are seeking a lover or companionship and the younger ones are desperate for money in order to better their lives. So all in all, both parties benefit from the relationship.

Sadly, there is a very dark side to sex work. A number of bar workers are HIV positive and yet they continue to work. Although bars usually require their dancers to undergo monthly health checks, many cases slip through undetected. You take a huge risk every time you sleep with a working boy or girl. Also, the age of those getting infected is constantly dropping. They might look young and healthy, but some may not even know they're infected, while others do and yet choose to continue working. Many of my co-workers have died from AIDS, having once been good-looking men with muscular bodies; but the disease ravaged them and reduced them to emaciated, stinking cadavers. Many died alone, rejected by their families. These were the very same families the dancers had built houses or bought cars for, and fed and clothed for years.

I firmly believe there is nothing wrong with the sex-for-sale business if all parties involved are consenting. I'm very much in favour of decriminalising prostitution and offering participants protection by the law. If a male sex worker is raped or abused we have a harder time than our female counterparts in getting assistance from healthcare providers or the authorities. In fact, for the most part, we don't even bother making a police report because we know it'll be a waste of time and energy—not to mention completely humiliating.

CHAPTER 14

When the going got tough, Sao's true colours came to light and I realised, much to my own detriment, that she was bad-tempered and ill-mannered. Her childhood was beset by poverty and abuse, which forced her as a teenager to work in Patpong. During the years she should've been completing secondary school, she sold her body and became a regular girl for a prominent businessman. She quickly took up drinking and drugs in the hope of numbing the ordeal of having her body pawed by strangers. She was especially fond of a drug known locally as *met mao*, or 'drunken pill'. When under its spell she felt no pain, so she'd pick up a blade or shard of glass and slice open her wrists and arms. Her body still bears testament to the number of times she spent harming herself in these trance-like states. Together, Sao and I occasionally used *ya ba*, which we smoked for the high aphrodisiac effect before we had sex. Thankfully, I never took it on a regular basis.

Sao's jealousy was overwrought, but I could have lived with this side of her personality—her hypocrisy disturbed me the most. She wasn't one for practising what she preached. She forbade me to drink and gamble while she would drunkenly gallivant off into the night with her male companions.

'You can't handle drink like I can. You have a weak spine,' she reasoned.

If Sao noticed that I so much as glanced at another woman she'd slap my face. One night a Japanese woman offered to buy me for 1,500 baht, but Sao wouldn't hear of it. She obnoxiously hurled profanities at the poor woman, sending her running in tears. It was ironic that in the past I'd been the violent and abusive partner. The boomerang of my previous actions had returned to me in the form of the supposedly 'fairer' sex.

Sao openly flirted with my male acquaintances as if to humiliate me. I continually reminded her, 'Marriage license or not, you are my woman and should treat me with the respect I deserve!' When confronted, she laughed in my face, retorting, 'These men are only good friends!' Good friends indeed. What woman would sit in her male friend's lap, pecking and hugging him in front of her boyfriend? Rumours trickled back that Sao was sleeping with other men behind my back. I was livid; I imagined her lovers laughing at me for being nothing more than putty in her hands.

I knew I was liable to hurt Sao if this continued—I needed to show her who was boss and if that meant resorting to violence then so be it. Luckily for her, fate intervened and Sao fell pregnant so I didn't beat her. Despite the fact I wasn't sure if the baby was mine, I was still happy. Given the fact I was trying my hand at 'ghost guiding'—bringing customers to bars in exchange for commissions, I believed I was in a better position to raise a child. The only drawback was that the mother was violent and manipulative. I chose to ignore that fact, however, for I desperately wanted to raise a family to show I'd done something worthwhile with my life. I took great comfort in the prospect of my child taking care of me in my old age. I was terrified of dying alone and destitute, and believed this child would provide security and a chance to make amends for the life of the child I'd already taken, as well as the son I'd lost.

While I was happy, Sao found pregnancy very difficult. She became even more unstable, and dramatically flew off the handle at the slightest provocation. She threatened that if I ever touched alcohol she'd throw herself under a bus. While I stayed sober, she smoked and drank her way through the pregnancy. I worried that the baby might be born handicapped.

The birth of my second son was a much more sedate affair than that involving Chuan. I didn't book a VIP room as I had neither the money nor the inclination to do so. Instead, Sao shared her room with several other new mothers. She treated what should've been a joyous event with an attitude that bordered on scorn. Our son Phot was born on 24 October 2006, without the fanfare he so deserved.

Ever the opportunist, Sao paraded Phot around her old workplaces in Patpong, collecting thousands of baht in gifts from her acquaintances. Sao wasn't naturally inclined to be motherly, but certainly played the game to her advantage. In a way I was relieved she was no longer pregnant and I didn't have to tread so softly. As soon as she was released from hospital, I went out to celebrate and heartily succumbed to the temptations of alcohol. But my behaviour was akin to a teenager rebelling against his strict mother. I reasoned that she'd be too busy minding the baby to have time to pounce on me for drinking.

I wasn't surprised when Sao informed me that a female restaurant/pub owner was interested in adopting our newborn. Phot was an attractive, pleasant baby who liked to wave his arms around in the air, jabbing his little balled-up fists at invisible targets. All who saw him remarked that he was surely a boxer in the making. I was convinced he was the reincarnation of my departed father—a pugilist to the core.

Wanting the baby desperately, the restaurateur badgered Sao for an answer. Sao asked if I wanted to give Phot a better life and I replied yes, but not by abandoning him for others to rear. I closed the matter, telling her it wasn't open for discussion.

One evening Sao went to visit friends. When she returned several hours later to find me drinking she became enraged. I tried to explain that I was a good provider in general and I deserved a treat on occasion—a well-worn excuse by now. There was no reasoning with Sao; she took Phot in her arms and stormed out.

I thought she was being a drama queen and would be back before long, but I didn't lay eyes on her for several weeks. My acquaintances divulged that she was telling people I was an irresponsible drunkard and she wanted nothing to do with me.

When I finally met her she matter-of-factly informed me, 'I've given Phot to the restaurateur. Your signature is needed on the adoption papers. They're waiting for you at a horse ranch in Khorat. Please go.'

It turned out, however, that Phot hadn't been adopted by the female restaurateur after all; she had instead brokered the deal for her brother and his wife. It later came to light that Sao had already given away two other children before Phot: a daughter she had with a Thai-African man and another son. Both were adopted by two bar owners in Pattaya. I suspected Sao made a substantial profit by selling our son to the wealthy ranch owners.

I was distraught over the loss of yet another child. Sao tried to offer comfort by assuring me, 'We did Phot a favour by giving him to a rich family. I want to go back to work—both of us will make lots of money since we are free of this burden.'

It disgusted me that she hadn't formed a bond with our baby and I began to wonder if she was actually capable of forming real relationships with anyone. She was a selfish, independent party girl and I had no idea what went on in her head. She was in her mid thirties when she gave birth to Phot, and yet she didn't realise her days of carefree partying were numbered. She lived for the moment, and it never occurred to her that there might come a time when she would need children to look after her.

I decided I'd had enough of Sao. I yelled, 'Burden? You destroyed my chance at having a family! I'll never forgive you! How could you not factor in my feelings when you decided to SELL Phot behind my back?'

Deep down I knew that his adoptive family could offer him a better life, but it bothered me that she didn't have his best interests at heart. She'd given him away only for the money.

She couldn't persuade me to go to Khorat to sign the papers. I didn't want my son to think I didn't care for him, so I refused to put my name to anything. In the end my hands were tied and there was little I could do to get Phot back. Had I shown up at the adoptive parents' house demanding the return of my son the 'influential' couple could have used force to make me more agreeable. How could I, a poor sex worker, ever win a battle against such rich and powerful people? Yes they could offer him a good life; but the fact is they practically stole my son and his own mother had been their main accomplice. So at four months old my precious Phot exited my life.

Sao stayed in contact with the adoptive parents but I've often wondered if her motives for remaining friends with them are sincere or if she is secretly plotting to blackmail them in the future. Anything is possible with Sao.

My HIV-positive friend Suthin took pity on me when he heard about Sao and Phot, and offered me a room in his apartment until I found alternative accommodation. I wasn't sure if I wanted to break up with Sao because it'd leave me homeless. But I had no desire to make things right between us again either. I took Suthin up on his offer and bought myself some time. I decided I'd stay in his apartment until I'd calmed down and could think clearly. The rent was generously paid for by a *farang* who owned two boy bars in Bangkok. Suthin had once worked for him and been his top boy before he fell ill. The apartment had two bedrooms, two bathrooms, and a kitchen/living area, so there was enough room for me to join his family. Suthin's three young children were under the age of six and his wife, Wilai, was pregnant as well.

When I moved in, the disease had begun to exact its toll and Suthin was no longer able to work. Before his *farang* boss came to his rescue, he'd worked as a security guard in a department store but found it too physically demanding and was forced to quit. I've no idea if his pregnant wife or any of the kids had contracted the disease.

I tried to pay my way and ease their load by buying food for them. A week after I moved in, Suthin happened to bump into Nuan. He sang my praises to her, telling her how well I was doing working as a part-time hustler and guide. He said I was making thousands of baht a night which was a wild exaggeration. These earnings ranged from 800 to 1,000 baht on average, and this was depending on how much I drank. Suthin told Nuan I'd taken a new lover and, exaggerating yet again, told her I loved Sao so much I was willing to even wash her underwear. Suthin was obviously trying to win Nuan back for me, and he certainly knew how to play her as apparently she was visibly upset by the news. He also took the liberty of arranging a reunion for us the following day.

I was nervous, but soon realised that I needn't have been because the second I saw Nuan she threw her arms around me and it was as if we'd never been apart. We slept together later that night and with that I got my family back.

Nuan confided that she hadn't been able to bear Chuan repeatedly begging her to take him to visit me. He couldn't understand why we were no longer together and Nuan was overcome with guilt at having taken her son away from his father.

I promised Nuan this time around things would be better. My work had always been a bone of contention between us but I assured her that she'd no longer have to lie to our son about my job. I was trying to leave prostitution behind by establishing myself as a guide in Patpong.

Nuan and Chuan moved into the apartment with Suthin's family and although I was overjoyed to have my family back, I still hadn't fully let go of Sao. I was travelling back and forth between Suthin's apartment and Sao's, servicing both women. Sao fluctuated between begging and threatening me, to make me leave Nuan. She began calling Nuan daily, screaming profanely at her down the phone in attempts to drive her away. Nuan, on the other hand, completely understood I wanted a second wife since she'd been the one to abandon me four years earlier. I found myself at a very confusing juncture; I didn't know whom to choose. I drank in order to postpone the decision-making, and my guide work suffered as a result. My friends advised me to choose Nuan over Sao as she was both the nicer person and a good mother to my child. They argued that I had no future with Sao, especially since Phot was out of the picture. Nuan finally won and I was hers alone.

At first I tried to hide from Nuan that I was drinking again. Within a month of reuniting I'd become careless and was returning home drunk regularly. I expected Nuan to admonish me, but strangely enough she said nothing. Instead, Suthin and Wilai took it upon themselves to gang up on me. They reproved me by calling me the nastiest names imaginable, especially when I returned home with no money. Conversely, when I returned loaded with cash and food they'd sing my praises. I'd clearly become nothing more than a cash cow to them. The disrespect and blatant insincerity they displayed had the positive side effect of drawing my family closer together. Nuan became irate when Wilai spoke ill of me in front of Chuan. She'd nicknamed the unappreciative couple 'the leeches', and felt that since I was feeding the entire household I deserved more respect. I was earning some money, but when it was divided amongst eight and an unborn, there wasn't much left over. I was under great pressure to make ends meet and having to contend with their criticisms didn't make matters any easier.

Nuan and I discussed the possibility of finding our own room but I was hesitant about leaving Suthin because of the kindness he'd shown when I needed help. One evening, Nuan came to see me at work carrying several bags, with Chuan dragging more behind her. She looked very upset. I'd called her earlier and asked her to bring me a change of clothing before I started work. She told me what had happened. Wilai walked into our room while Nuan was packing the clothes for me.

'So you're leaving us now. What good timing!' she said.

'Chai needs a change of clothing. You'd do the same for Suthin . . .' she paused and then said, 'It might not hurt you if just for once you people showed Chai some gratitude.'

'Don't act so high and mighty. We'll pay you both back when we're good and ready.'

'I doubt you leeches could ever repay us, even in your next life. When was the last time your dying husband even left the house? And what can you do, you helpless waddling sow!'

With that, Nuan packed up all of our belongings and stormed out of the apartment.

Throughout Nuan's story, Chuan nodded his head in agreement; he seemed proud of his mother for having stood up to Wilai. I was just relieved that we didn't have to go back to that stifling, depressing atmosphere ever again.

You are probably expecting me to tell you that Nuan, Chuan and I all lived happily ever after; but I am afraid that, as with Lin, this was not the case. I continued to drink heavily and the majority of my money went towards feeding my addiction. Drunken guides weren't much in demand in Patpong so our income quickly evaporated. Money once again had become the main source of conflict between us. Nuan and I began to fight constantly.

I was sometimes drunk for days straight. I still hadn't realised how destructive a force alcohol was. It had been a major player in nearly every disaster that befell me, and yet I saw it as the solution to all my problems. It was a trusty crutch; always at hand to support me through troublesome times. It'd never once occurred to me that I might be an alcoholic—the very notion seemed ridiculous. I mean, my whole family drank, and so did most of the villagers—it was something everyone did. But on some level, I realised that most of the pain and hurt I was responsible for had actually been inflicted when I was intoxicated.

You have to hit rock bottom before you can begin climbing out of a hole. It's only when you're lying flat on your back that you can see just how far you've fallen. I'd been falling for a long time, and all the time suspected that I must be nearing the bottom; yet I hastened the process all the more by my destructive behaviour.

One Friday afternoon Nuan called to see me while I was working. She was looking for money because there was no food left. I waved some banknotes in front of her face tauntingly and then snatched them away.

'Fat chance,' I said.

We'd had a huge row about my drinking two days earlier and I hadn't returned home since. I expected Nuan to start a fight but she simply shrugged her shoulders and walked off. She knew well there was little chance of me giving her anything when I was in that kind of mood; besides, she had to pick Chuan up from school. I stumbled home and destroyed everything in sight. I don't know what I was thinking. Perhaps the problem was that I wasn't thinking at all.

When I had thoroughly demolished our room, I met up with two of my friends and continued my tipple-fest until the bars were closed. By this stage, my friend Nitthi and I were so off our faces we had no idea where we were. My other friend, Sophon, was also drunk but later on was able to recount the near-fatal assault that led to my current hospitalisation. Sophon recalled that Arun, a Cambodian acquaintance, was walking over to us. He was clearly high, having smoked an ungodly amount of amphetamines, capping it with bucket-loads of beer. He was brimming with energy and, earlier on, was intentionally bothering passers-by in the *soi* for entertainment. He couldn't stand still for a second; his body was twitching uncontrollably as he jumped up and down, shouting like a crazy man. My two friends and I were passed out on a white couch, in an open-air bar at the entrance to Soi Twilight, when Arun approached us. He began poking Nitthi, trying to irritate him and awaken him from his slumber. Nitthi didn't find it funny and kept pushing Arun away. But Arun persistently continued to poke his ribs. I angrily ordered Arun to stop and to get lost.

My little comment started a full-scale brawl. I had loaned Arun money in the past, and I reminded him of this to gain leverage in the argument. Instead of putting him in his place, my reference to money was taken as an insult. He suddenly dove at me, slapping me across the face. I folded like a deck of cards, but managed to drag myself to my feet. I was intent on giving Arun a black eye and swung my fist hard but missed. Arun then kicked me in the stomach and it was at that point I blacked out.

CHAPTER 15

I've now been sent home from hospital, yes, home; and I've never been so happy to have one to go to. My happiness, when compared with the fear I experienced in hospital, has indeed been a catalyst preventing me from returning to my former weaknesses.

The only thing that trumped my physical injuries in terms of pain was the look of terror in my son's eyes whenever he came to visit. When I awoke from the coma, I was in a state of delirium and didn't remember Nuan or Chuan visiting me. The doctors told me that they came daily, but the memories of their visits faded as soon as they exited the ward. One of my first clear memories was of Chuan, though. He was standing next to me, with his bone-white knuckles gripping the bedrails tightly. He didn't say a word, as if too scared; instead he slipped his hand into mine as he fought back the tears. He looked thin and pale; he'd obviously been deeply affected on seeing me close to death. The worry in his eyes confirmed my worst fears—I mightn't pull through and, even if I did, who knew what difficulties lay ahead. Both Chuan and Nuan were struggling to cope with my hospitalisation. Their eyes, furrowed brows and behaviour belied all. They worried about how to ease my worries, but ironically, this caused me to worry all the more.

As I stared into my son's red, sorrow-filled eyes, I could see the legacy of pain and uncertainty I'd handed down to him. It was too much for any child to bear. He was silently imploring me to stop hurting him and his mother. I squeezed his hand reassuringly, trying to mouth the words 'I'm sorry'; but the pain was too great and they stuck in my throat.

I was deeply sorry for having subjected him to such an ordeal. I imagined my funeral and wondered how my death would affect him. He'd surely be devastated, but was it possible that in a small way he'd be secretly relieved? I wondered if he'd recall any happy memories from our lives together, or have something good to say about me at all. My son's brokenness had more of a healing power over me than all the medication in the hospital combined. I determined that if I ever made it out of the ward, I'd be a better father to Chuan.

'I will live. I will live', I chanted to myself. My son's face faded as I fell into a deep sleep.

During the early weeks in hospital, various friends helped Nuan piece together the events that unfolded on the fateful night of my attack. Apparently, after I fell unconscious, Arun attacked me mercilessly. Sophon, being relatively sober, tried to defend me but Arun dealt him a swift blow that sent him hurtling to the ground. Sophon stepped back and, perhaps to justify his cowardice, convinced himself that since Arun and I'd been conversing in Khmer, we must be related. That made it a family feud in which an outsider, like Sophon, shouldn't intervene.

Sophon wasn't the only coward; I was surrounded by them. I found out afterwards several other people witnessed the bloody assault but not one had come to my rescue. They either didn't care or were fearful of the consequences of getting involved. I haven't exactly earned any loyal protectors over the years, that's for sure. I just hope that one day the people who pretended not to see the savage attack on me won't find their loved ones falling victim to similar indifference.

As I lay in a crumpled heap, Arun moved with careful precision, making sure that every blow he dealt my body inflicted maximum damage. He took a brief break to assess his handiwork before launching another merciless round. Pulling me to my feet, he cupped his hand under my chin and began bouncing my head off electricity poles and walls. He then ripped off my shirt and dragged me along the road. The uneven surface ripped my chest, face and arms, tearing layers of skin. He then stomped on my head with his boots, and still not wholly satisfied with his efforts, dragged me up the stairs of a nearby bar and released me, gleefully watching as I tumbled downwards like a sack of rice. After this coup de grâce, he left me to die facedown on the road.

I could scarcely believe Arun was responsible for nearly killing me. We'd been drinking buddies when we worked as go-go boys, but he started taking drugs and was never the same again. The police had arrested him numerous times, and his rap sheet was a veritable litany of charges involving either assault or minor drug possession. The police had him over a barrel at this point and threatened to prosecute again unless he participated in drugs stings. All the go-go boys knew what he was doing and so naturally didn't trust him. He brazenly asked for a 'loan' to buy drugs, supposedly for one of these stings. He was clearly lying though, and was only looking to fund his habit. When I refused him, he cursed my name and stormed off.

Arun disappeared and it was several months before he resurfaced. When he did, it was as if nothing had happened between us; he was civil, so I assumed he'd put our differences behind him. I was clearly wrong though; he'd been nursing a grudge and was waiting for an opportunity to exact revenge. I should've known he was a loose cannon, and that he was capable of anything.

Arun openly boasted that he'd fought as a child soldier for Heng Samrin. He claimed he'd been part of a movement backed by Vietnam and the Soviet Union to overthrow Pol Pot and bring an end to the Khmer Rouge's regime. He loved to brag about his exploits, even several times claiming to have eaten human flesh in order to survive.

It's hard to imagine, but it would take 12 hours before I was found lying unconscious. During the morning the *soi* is deserted. Being home to bars and businesses, it doesn't come to life until late in the afternoon. An acquaintance happened upon me and, spotting me lying facedown, didn't pay much attention because he presumed I was just sleeping off yet another night on the town. He shook his head disapprovingly and was ready to walk by. It was only as he came closer that he realised all was not right. I was lying unnaturally still and my limbs were placed at awkward angles. He tried to shake me awake but I wouldn't budge. So he turned me over and the sight of my swollen, battered body sent him reeling. I was completely limp and he was sure I was dead, so he called the police and paramedics. Amidst blaring sirens and flashing lights, I was loaded into the back of an ambulance. They rushed me to the nearest hospital which happened to be an expensive private facility. On seeing I had no identification on me and that I might not have insurance, they refused to admit me, despite the fact I could've died. So I was reloaded into the ambulance and sent to the nearest public hospital instead. I have no notion of any of this as I only barely regained consciousness four days after I was admitted.

Nuan told me she hadn't recognised the bloated, shaved-headed man whom the nurse insisted was me. I was wrapped in so many bandages I looked like a mummy. It was only when Nuan lifted the bedcovers and took a peek at my feet that she believed the disfigured shape was me.

When I finally came to, it was as though I was in a waking coma. I was incoherent and confused. I had no idea where I was. I was convinced I was in a different hospital—one I had been admitted to in the past. I suppose I remembered that the staff in that hospital were always very kind to me so subconsciously I wished I was there. When Nuan insisted I wasn't in that hospital, I became irate. I was convinced the staff in the current hospital were inferior and insisted I be transferred immediately. I was vocal about my misgivings, accusing the nurses of looking down on me and mistreating me. My belligerent behaviour definitely didn't earn me any friends and eventually caused the nurses to shun me.

When I regained some strength, Nuan recounted how she'd found me. After I vandalised our room and stormed back to the bar in a huff, she returned home with Chuan to find the landlord angrily blocking the entrance.

'Your belongings are in a garbage bag. Don't ever come here again. Tell your good-for-nothing husband he isn't welcome either,' he yelled.

Nuan was distraught. She rang a friend of hers who runs a small laundry shop asking if she could offer temporary refuge as she was completely broke. Thankfully, Nuan's friend's husband was working in Lopburi at the time and felt it'd be good for his wife to have company. So Nuan and Chuan were made welcome. Nuan tearfully told her how I'd let her down yet again, saying that if she'd known I was still addicted to alcohol she would never have reconciled with me.

Nuan promised to earn her keep working in the laundry and helping out with household chores. She called to a grocery store in Soi Twilight to ask if the owner, Auntie Pin, knew of my whereabouts. I often bought liquor from her store so she knew me well. Auntie Pin replied, 'I'm sure Chai is just drunk somewhere close by. Don't worry, dear. He probably hasn't stumbled too far.'

Arun had attacked me in the early hours of Sunday morning. By Monday evening, when Nuan still hadn't received word of my whereabouts, she collected Chuan from school and searched Silom looking for me.

Passing through the *soi*, a good-humoured grilled squid vendor stopped Nuan to ask her how I was. Nuan knew the woman vaguely and was surprised when she enquired, 'Is your husband getting better? Only good merit will get him up and walking again.'

'What are you talking about?' Nuan asked.

'Didn't you know he was attacked? They say his skull was cracked open. There's very little chance of him . . .' The vendor managed to catch herself before disclosing the seriousness of the situation. But her body language had said it all.

Nuan frantically asked what hospital I was in and sped off to find me.

Since the Patpong 'tell-a-friend' communication services work better than the telephone, Sao caught wind of my assault and made an unexpected visit to the hospital. She disclosed that she'd been struggling to make ends meet while working as a bar girl. She said that she needed me and implored me to return and help support her. I saw no reason to get back with her, but still kept these thoughts to myself. She'd given away Phot, so I would have to be insane to return to such a negative situation. Rather than risk an unpleasant confrontation, I just told her that we'd talk once I got better. I never heard from her again, so presumably she got the message.

My time in hospital provided both Nuan and me with ample opportunity to talk things over. She knew Sao had visited me but refused to fight with her. Nuan told me I was free to go back to her if I wanted. Instead, I chose to give our small family another chance and asked her to do the same. I reassured her that after my release from hospital I wanted to really change this time—no more false starts.

All in all, Nuan has been fantastic; she managed to juggle her daily visits to the hospital with raising Chuan. She insisted the police should take action and put pressure on them to bring Arun to justice. I respected her more and more with each passing day and began to realise how fortunate I was to have her in my life.

After she gathered as much information about the attack as possible, she headed to the police station and filed an official complaint. The police officer working the case called Sophon in for questioning. He asked why he hadn't done more to stop the assault, or at least taken me to the hospital after it. Sophon told him that he thought it best to let the bar owners take care of the matter. But a simple phone call to the police would've sufficed and he didn't even do that.

I really can't understand his logic at all. I was attacked at around 5am and he had plenty of time to go get help; instead, he just left me for dead. When the ambulance finally came, there was a huge crowd of onlookers gathered to see what all the commotion was. We have a saying, *Thai mung*, which translates as 'a Thai stare'. It's a cultural thing. If an accident occurs everyone rushes to peer at what has happened; few do anything to help the situation though. It's as if an accident is a welcome distraction from the monotony of their humdrum existence, by providing them with something new to gossip about. I must be careful not to become embittered about this outlook though. In reality it was my own fault I ended up in hospital. It's about time I stopped blaming others and started taking responsibility for my actions. The indifferent world won't readily lend me a helping hand, that's for sure.

My doctor initially told Nuan there was very little chance I'd regain consciousness and even if I did, I'd be a vegetable at best. My recovery exceeded the doctor's expectation though. Meanwhile, Nuan was becoming increasingly frustrated with the police and their failure to take action. In a moment of utter disgust, she accused them of allowing scores of known criminals roam the streets, and even brought up the issue of my father's murder. She reproached them for failing to deliver justice and said that she hoped my case would be different. She warned them that she'd take the matter to the Crime Suppression Bureau if the local Metropolitan Police didn't prove good. Nuan was clearly very upset about the attack and was worried Arun would come after her and Chuan. To be fair, he was completely deranged, so there was no telling what he was capable of. Nuan told the police that she'd already been disappointed by them once, and that she wouldn't settle for such incompetence a second time.

It was over seven years since my father was murdered; my sister Nit took the matter to the police department a few years back but the commander responsible for investigation asked her to withdraw her complaint. He assured her if she did as he requested he would personally see to it the murderers were brought to justice. She was afraid of him and backed down but she never heard a peep from him again. Nuan refused to be bullied, reasoning if she left the police to their own devices and didn't continue to put them under pressure then justice wouldn't be served. Thankfully, her insistence paid off.

A friend informed me that Arun was working in front of a hotel in another district of Bangkok. His working outside of his usual domain was obviously an attempt to keep a low profile. I passed this information on to the officer working my case and he immediately issued a warrant for Arun's arrest. He was to be charged with physical assault but I believe it should have been attempted murder. That would be difficult to prove though. Arun protested his innocence, insisting that we'd been friends for a long time and he'd no reason to harm me. Arun is currently in the prison awaiting trial.

When I was first admitted to the hospital I underwent a blood transfusion, receiving six litres in total. I was bleeding inside my skull due to the head injuries I'd sustained and the volume of blood was putting a lot of pressure on my brain. I had to have several operations that involved opening my skull to relieve the pressure. I received 100 stitches to my head alone.

My medical bills amounted to over 100,000 baht. But Nuan begged the hospital to cover my costs under the governmental 30-baht healthcare scheme and thankfully, they agreed.

During our many heartfelt conversations, Nuan and I would discuss our future plans for raising Chuan. Nuan worries that he'll one day become a bar boy, a kind of karmic punishment for the fact that it was bar-boy earnings that fed and clothed him during infancy. Indeed, he is highly familiar with the sights and sounds of Soi Twilight as he and Nuan used to call to collect me after my shifts. He could easily have been led to believe that being a go-go boy is about having fun and partying.

We both agreed to find alternative work, and planned to save up money to put a deposit on a modest house far away from the bar scene and red-light districts. Soi

Patpong and Soi Twilight might feel like home to me, but they're simply not suitable places in which to raise children.

After the attack, a few bar owners kindly sent small amounts of money to help with expenses. These men were never part of my drinking circle yet I consider them true friends for their kindness. They were always the ones warning me to curtail my spending and to watch my behaviour. I can't thank them enough for the kindness they showed me.

This might not make sense to Westerners, but I believe that the terrible karma I committed in my past lives rendered me incapable of seeing the error of my ways in this one. We Thais say 'karma has thrown a veil over my head'. Until I've paid for my former sins, I'm fated to stumble blindly on through the obstacle course of my present life. No amount of warning could lift my karmic veil and keep me from going off the rails.

Thais like all kinds of fortune-telling; be it palm-reading, tarot cards, horoscopes, or dream analysis. I've visited different fortune-tellers down through the years and all of them have confirmed that I'm shadowed by a karmic hex, and burdened by a large amount of karmic baggage.

My last reading prior to the attack was done by a man who had a table next to a charity foundation that is best known for their rescue work. I sometimes donated money to this foundation to make merit. The money is used to buy coffins for people who don't have anyone to cover the expenses of a funeral. In most cases, the dead do have friends or relatives but for some reason these people don't want to take responsibility for them. There are several such foundations and they employ 'volunteers' to race around in pick-up trucks, ensuring they are the first to arrive at the scene of an accident, murder, or some other type of tragedy. They get paid for every body that is taken either to a hospital, morgue, or to the foundation. On occasion, the jewellery and wallets of the injured or dead disappear en route. For this reason their activities are jokingly referred to as body-snatching. Since employees work on a commission basis, some rival foundations have been known to fight over bodies, especially during major disasters. Sometimes employees will ignore the rules of the road and actually cause accidents themselves in their haste to get to the scene of an accident.

You may wonder why I bother to donate to such operations. Well, in their defence, they are often willing to do some of the less desirable jobs like cleaning up after a road accident, jobs at which even the police baulk. These foundations also donate to prisoners annually and help to hospitalise the dangerous or mentally deranged among them; and these are just a few of the many other good deeds they perform.

Whenever I visited the foundation, I handed my donation over to the officer on duty and he issued a receipt which would be pasted on one of the empty coffins. Dozens of these coffins are lined up side by side, and there are gory pictures of all types of horrific accidents adorning the walls. Little did I know I'd soon come very close to filling one of these coffins.

It's normal practice to have one's fortune read immediately after merit making, so I obligingly visited the nearby fortune-teller. He asked for my date of birth and also for the exact time. He wrote the figures down and pored over them for a few moments, while carrying out some mental calculations. A shadow passed over his face.

'This year will be a very bad year for you,' he said.

He instructed me to go to a certain Chinese shrine and worship three specific gods otherwise a great tragedy would befall me. He also commented that I was unable to return to my place of birth for some reason. I admitted I was a former juvenile delinquent and had offended many people in my village. What followed was a tirade of ethical mumbo-jumbo, the essence of which was that I needed to learn how to control my temper and be more patient. Had he not issued such a self-righteous lecture I might have taken his ominous predictions more seriously.

There wasn't really a need for me to visit fortune-tellers. All my life, the people closest to me were already warning that I was travelling along a self-destructive path. Even then I knew they spoke the truth but I was blinded by pride. Hell, even my own son rebuked me when I drank. If he was in a bad mood or was exceptionally unruly he'd dismiss my corrections, telling me that I was a bad example and therefore not worth listening to.

Having barely made it out of the hospital in one piece my perspective on life has been irrevocably altered. All deities, karma, and mortal beings aside, I'm finally coming to the conclusion that I am responsible for my own actions. I feel that if my life is to change for the better it's up to me alone to steer it in the right direction. I can't allow myself to obsess over the past, nor find scapegoats in the various people I've crossed paths with; neither my bad friends, nor my abusive teacher, nor my first *farang* client. What good will it do for me to point the finger at these ghosts? I may not be able to rewrite history, but I can change my attitude towards life now to secure a good future.

It's clear that drink most certainly doesn't suit me. Abstinence is only the beginning; I have a lot of work to do. I've been blindly blaming others for all my failings, waging war on a faceless adversary only to discover that the greatest adversary is none other than myself—I am my own worst enemy. It's only now I'm ready to lay down my weapons and make peace with myself, while at the same time vanquishing the demons which have haunted me for so many years.

EPILOGUE

A year has passed since I last wrote, and I thought it was time to wrap up my thoughts. The reason I have waited till now is that I thought I still lacked a proper conclusion to my story. Now, at last, I believe I can provide one.

I'm back on the streets. This time it's different though. I'm able to walk and am still in my right mind, remarkably enough. I can also talk, laugh and wheel and deal once more. However, I think the gods have short-circuited me since my accident: even if I wanted to, I simply couldn't drink as much as I used to. My body gets tired and just won't permit me; it's as if the gods have made a divine pronouncement over my life saying, *mai owe laew*, that is 'no more'. This, I reckon, is the payment that has been required of me for their good will in keeping me alive. But I'm even forbidden to drink coffee—they really do have a sense of humour I think. So I resort to eating sweets as a substitute for these forbidden luxuries. I suck and suck, as if to swallow all my cravings for the destruction I once poured so copiously down my throat. As I walk I hope that I might continue swallowing these yearnings in future. If I overstep the ordained bounds, I will further damage my brain, which surely would signal the end. I'll actually become the vegetable the doctors had predicted I'd be. So, I obey the doctors, pray, suck my sweets and, most significantly, I do not drink.

Bar owners, bar boys and even the cops are amazed by my transformation; though it's going to take time to prove to them that this is not an act. It's the real deal this time. One policeman affectionately tapped me on the head the other day querying why I wasn't drunk yet. He laughed incredulously when I smiled politely and informed him I wasn't fond of the bottle anymore. He actually seemed visibly relieved—one less problem to have to deal with. Yes, indeed, it's going to take some time for others to accept that I'm a different man; why it's nearly impossible to believe it myself.

I have a new lease on life; a second chance, or perhaps it's actually my third, fourth, or fifth—the point is, this time I'm willing to take it and keep it. My wife insists I've had a brain transplant and jokes that the doctors secretly changed my brain in the process of saving my life. Whatever happened, I've been saved and have a new way of thinking. My wife shakes her head and smiles; she even laughs and seems genuinely proud of me—it's been a long time since I felt that from her. She commends me for being a good father and a real man, and she's enjoying getting to know her new husband at last. She even reports that my extreme makeover is somewhat akin to having an affair with another man. The drunken unreliable one left home and a better model returned in his place.

The doctors didn't want me to check out of hospital; they actually refused permission, but I insisted so they eventually conceded. We had to eat and I had to make a baht or two for my family; they were relying on me. Even though my head and a part of my face looked ugly and lopsided for the first few months—a side effect of the assault and operations—I just hid the worst deformities with a hat. On the day I returned to work, I shaved, dressed and put on my sunglasses to hide any other appearance of damage. Then I did what I had to do. I hit the streets.

Yes, I am a streetwalker, but one with a difference. Let me explain.

As I've already outlined, when things got bad in the go-go industry, I had to take to the streets to earn a living. I poured my English skills and sales abilities into being a ghost guide, and plied this sideline trade around the same areas I'd formerly worked in for years —this time in front of the stage instead of on it.

A ghost guide is a self-employed, non-official tour guide whom tourists are warned best to avoid. But let me tell you, if you come to Patpong, where are you going to find an official tour guide who will bring you to a place that doesn't legally exist? And let's say you did; would they know the business as I do? Could they guide you to a good bar, find you a good boy, bring you to the places that sell the best food, or even protect you from scams as I can? While I would warn against being exploited by the many touts who roam the streets looking for gullible tourists to scam, I am *not* a tout. I am a ghost guide! And in a place that does not exist, amongst men and women who do not sell their bodies. But just tell me what you need and, for a price, I'll get it.

In the past, my short stints at 'guiding' didn't work well. Who was going to trust a drunken obnoxious character to transport them through a labyrinth of red-light delights? I stumbled blindly around the streets, slurring my words, attempting to conduct business by hassling and haranguing would-be customers.

An epiphany of sorts came to me as I lay in my hospital bed shackled by fear, a fear of what my future entailed. Marvellously, a ray of hope illuminated my thoughts with questions I felt I could answer for a change. What if I was to once more be a guide, a non-drunken, respectable guide? Couldn't I then support my family? Wouldn't this be a somewhat suitable profession for a man my age? As if presented with a magical saw, I started to cut away my shackles one by one, and watched in delight as they seemed to drop from my withered limbs. As the weight fell, my convictions grew; and with that, so did my enthusiasm to get back into the ring in readiness to slug it out if need be. Yes, I had been knocked down many times, but I had never been counted out. I wasn't out of the fight, so long as I could get to my feet and punch my way through to victory; and I would do this by cleaning myself up and becoming more presentable. I could win; I could live. I could earn enough to support the others that depended on me. With that vision, I packed my few belongs and said goodbye to the multitude of sad faces in that overcrowded ward of misery.

Admittedly, that gloomy ward provided some of the best schooling I've ever had. Lying in that bed allowed me to reflect on my wretched past, to see how checkered it is with huge monuments to failure; and this served to teach me that there were better paths to be sought. I secretly thanked God for tying me to a bed of pain and uncertainty. It was exactly what was needed to exact a transformation. I was so grateful heading out the swinging doors to whatever future awaited me.

It's not been easy, but it's been easier than I imagined. I don't have to answer to anyone; I make money daily and I'm able to take days off whenever I wish.

Basically, the way ghost-guiding works is that I persuade five tourists to go to a bar that offers sex shows or the like. I tell them the bar charges 500 baht per drink and each person is required to buy at least one. In reality though, bars usually charge patrons 300 baht a drink which includes a cover charge for watching shows. Additional costs may be incurred by tourists if a performer talks to them and the tourist purchases them a drink. After we're done with the bar for the evening, whatever I was able to skim on overcharge goes straight into my wallet.

Tourists who visit girl or boy bars these days are more savvy. They exchange information with each other on the Internet, so commission-making is a bit difficult. If I can't con money from overcharged drink prices, at least I usually score 100 baht in commission per person if I bring them to a go-go bar in Soi Twilight. The managers of these venues give me a coupon with one signature per client which is redeemable at the end of the night. Several bars refuse to pay, claiming some of the clients are not new customers. Other bars are more than willing to pay though, no matter what the circumstances.

One oddity of the job is that I am fined 100 baht every month by the police for pestering tourists. This doesn't mean I'm terrified of being arrested each month. It's an unofficial arrangement whereby a police officer simply pays me a visit and the 'fine' is handed over without ado. To me, it's a friendly business arrangement and we're all happy. 100 baht is nothing compared to how much I can make daily. I'm harmless to them; therefore, we can co-exist contentedly.

Each ghost guide has his own territory, and on Silom Road alone there's a seemingly endless amounts of them. My domain is Soi Twilight. When tourists want me to show them woman bars I do so; if they want to go to go-go boy, I only take them to the places that are straightforward about their commission policy. I don't necessarily bring them to the bars where the best-looking boys or the most exciting shows are available, but I go to where I can make good deals for myself. If I need to work in someone else's territory, I greet them with a *wai* and ask politely for permission to 'invade' their world. I show them respect, and in turn, they generally do the same to me.

I knew I could make a success of this line of work as I had connections with the majority of bar owners and business proprietors in the area. Although it's taken time to convince them I was capable, their need for clients prompted them to eventually cooperate. I wasn't initially confident in my ability to persuade would-be customers to go to the places I had a verbal agreement with. However I easily developed the skills I needed to gain the confidence of tourists. On my very first night at having a go as a sober ghost guide I fortunately did meet some customers. I took them to a show where they seemed to enjoy themselves and I made good commissions on the drinks, even on my own soft drinks. Every night thereafter, it has been the same story. Sometimes I even have three sets of customers in one evening. I dress well, eat properly, and my appearance is improving because at last I am happy and productive. After a night of work, I head home and hand over my well-earned cash to my beloved family. I then eat a home-cooked meal and afterwards, look over at my sleeping son with joy, before curling up with my wife and sleeping the sleep of the contented.

There are times when it's a struggle for sure; I'd be lying if I said otherwise. However, I believe that if I remain sober and continue doing what I am doing, things will continue to improve.

I realise that the work I do isn't exactly legal, or totally honest; but it's safer for me and my family, and even for the customers, than any alternative. I might lie to make money from the overcharge, but I don't really consider this a rip-off. I feel I give people a fair deal; after all, relatively speaking, they actually pay very little for the sex shows and for my services as a guide. There are even occasions when there is no sex involved. For example, I sometimes accompany tourists for beautiful seafood meals, or go see the local temples—who knows, maybe some day I'll be able to qualify as a real tour guide.

Another thing I'm grateful for is that I don't have to lie about my family anymore; I have a wife and a son and I can be proud of them, as they are of me.

All right, I understand that this may sound syrupy compared to my life of old; and some of you may have wanted me to go on further into the debauchery, but I no longer want it. I've shared what was needed in order to move on—and I thank you for wading through the horrors with me. A gentleman in an insane asylum, when questioned as to why he kept banging his head against the wall, replied that it felt good when he stopped. Unlike him, I no longer need to fluctuate between extremes of pleasure and pain to feel good—I'm done! I can finally say that what I now feel is genuine happiness, and not the kind that's simulated by a head banging against a wall.

I carry deep within me a dream to retire one day in the countryside with my family where we can fish, plant rice, and live naturally; and there I can end my life where I really should have started it. First things first though, we will buy the modest house my wife and I discussed when I was in the hospital.

Finally, to you the reader, whoever you are, if you happen to come to Soi Patpong or Soi Twilight, don't be afraid to look me up and see for yourself how I'm doing. You'll recognise me as the short, dark-skinned fellow, 41 years of age and smiling brightly at you, probably saying, 'Handsome man, where you from, would you like to see bar, club, show, or you want drink sir? I can help you!

'Come with me! Oh Germany? I love Germans they are kind people, good heart! You make good time? Have good time with me! I am good guide!'